Raw
Feeding
from
A to Z

An Introduction to Raw Feeding for Crazy Dog Lovers Like Me

An Update to 'A Novice's Guide to Raw Feeding'

Kimberly Gauthier, Dog Nutrition Blogger Keep the Tail Wagging®

The Legal Stuff

CONTACT INFORMATION

Kimberly Gauthier Keep the Tail Wagging®

Marysville, Washington 98271

W: http://www.keepthetailwagging.com

E: kimberly@keepthetailwagging.com

SOCIAL MEDIA

Facebook: Keep the Tail Wagging

Instagram: @RawFeederLife

YouTube: Kimberly Gauthier

TikTok: @RawFeederLife

Newslsetter: KeepTheTailWagging.com/Newsletter

Podcasts: Girls with Dogs and The Alternative Dog Moms

Dedication

When I first published this book, I dedicated it to my dogs, present and past, and my life partner. Little did I know I was three years away from losing my canine doppelgänger, Sydney, and five years away from losing Scout.

I dedicate this book to Sydney and Scout. One dog gave me the strength and the patience to become a multi-dog home. She was always calm in a crazy dog storm that was often our life with dogs. And one dog gave me joy daily, even when he was going through cancer treatments.

Having dogs makes every day happier, helps me sleep better, and inspires me to do better, to keep learning, and to put their quality of life before my breaking heart.

I will miss our daily hugs, their enthusiasm for food, the way Sydney always fell to the ground like a fainting goat whenever we went outside, and how Scout always gave me 20 sloppy kisses.

I'll meet you both (along with Jackson, Riley, and Blue) at the bridge.

About the Author

In my youth, I loved dogs, journaling, and clothes. I wanted to be a photo journalist or something in the fashion industry. My mother told me to get a business degree and turn the rest into a hobby.

I became a corporate accountant and started a personal blog about my dogs.

Today, I write about raw feeding and raising dogs naturally, sharing what I learn as I navigate this journey using Google, holistic veterinarians, and my fellow dog lovers as a guide.

I live in the Pacific Northwest with our dogs, a cat, and my better half.

Kimberly Gauthier

Forward

When I'm not scheduling therapy dogs for various animal-assisted therapeutic services, blogging, or playing around with my two Goldendoodles – Harley and Jaxson, I can usually be found reading/ researching all I can about dog health and welfare. A large degree of interest in that category is nutrition. I love to learn as much as I can about a diet that will complement their metabolism, protect their gut, and help maintain a healthy weight - which, when combined, will possibly grant them longevity here with me!

The pet blogging space affords me a limitless directory of pet parent professionals specializing in all subject matters related to animals. Regarding nutrition, supplements, and overall care of dogs, Kimberly Gauthier is on my A list to connect with and discuss how best to overcome those challenges.

I've known Kimberly since the indoor/outdoor pet water fountain invention! Ten years ago, we started following each other's pet blogs. It's been pure joy to watch her evolution from writing about her daily dog mom life to becoming "one voice in an ocean of voices" (her words) in the world of Raw Feeding dogs!

Her first book, "A Novice's Guide to Raw Feeding for Dogs," was not only a biblical reference to those who were plowing their fields in the life of a raw feeder, but it was an easy read for those of us who knew nothing, yet were curious and unaware of where to begin. When this book was first published, I was thirsty to learn more about a cleaner, healthier way to feed my dogs. Not equipped (both logistically and realistically) to be a raw feeder, I still found so much value in learning how to incorporate broths and proteins. Chapters hold their segregated content, which makes it great for navigating back and forth for re-reads.

"Keeping it Raw," her 2nd book, was loaded with questions "from" pet parents, which she answered to "share" with other pet parents. The format of this book was informative and also encouraging to me. Although I am still not a raw feeder – what I have learned from my friendship with Kimberly, her blog, newsletter, and books is that I can be the best "raw feeder – adjacent" pet parent for my Doodles.

Over time I have become an educated novice with the inclusion of fresh, human, healthy additions to their diet. Quickly I noticed energy level increases and a reduction (not complete eradication) in environmental allergies and seasonal ear infections. I attribute much of this to Kimberly sharing her extensive knowledge in layman's terminology.

Kimberly writes from the heart. She shares the good, the bad, and even the very ugly about this journey she still believes she is on. An avid reader, what she doesn't know, she will research until she does. Obsessed with the truth, she is like a dog with a bone (#punintended) until she's comfortable with the answers she seeks.

I'm looking forward to placing this latest book on my reference shelf right next to her other two. Whether you feed raw, air-dried, freeze-dried, or kibble – if you want to give your dog all that you can to ensure his/her days here on earth are healthy, happy, and plentiful (to the best of our abilities), then I highly recommend you clear some space on your reading shelf, grab a highlighter, order her books and plan to be immersed, engaged, and excited with each page.

Cathy C. Bennet, Groovy Goldendoodles

Contents

The Legal Stuff ii

Dedication iv

About the Author v

Forward vi

A - An Introduction to Raw Feeding 3

B - Balance, Bacteria, Behavior, and Raw Dog Food 25

C - Cost, Calcium, Carnivores, and Raw Dog Food 29

D - Disease, Dehydrated Food, Dog Dishes, and Dog Treats for Raw Fed Dogs 34

E - Eggs, Education, Evidence, and Raw Feeding 39

F - Fear, Fermentation, Fish and Fish Oil, Fasting, and Raw Feeding ... 44

G - Gut Health, Green Tripe, Guidelines and Raw Feeding 49

H - Holistic Veterinarians and Raw Feeding 53

I - Introducing a Raw Fed Dog to a New Veterinarian 56

J - Joint Health, Canine Arthritis, and Raw Feeding 58

K - Knowledge, Kicked Out, Kibble, and Raw Feeding 61

L - Liver, Liver Health, and Raw Feeding 65

M - Models of Raw Feeding for Dogs 67

N - Natural Vitamins, New Proteins, and Raw Feeding 74

O - Organ Meat, Offal, and Raw Feeding 78

P - Pork, Parasites, Pancreas, and Raw Feeding 81

Q - Quality Brands, Questions, and Raw Feeding 85

R - Recreational Bones, Raw Meaty Bones, and Raw Feeding 87

S - Supplements and Raw Feeding 90

T - Transitioning Your Partner to Raw Feeding 92

U - Understanding Your Dog and Raw Feeding 95

V - Vaccinations, Vegetables (and Fasting), and Raw Feeding 98

W - Warming Foods, Cooling Foods, and Raw Feeding 105

X - Examining Dog Poop and Raw Feeding... 110

Y - YouTube Channels for Raw Feeders... 113

Z - The Zen of a Full Freezer, Buying a Freezer, and Forgetting to Thaw Raw Dog Food.. 115

IF A DOG WON'T EAT RAW 120

DIY BONE BROTH... 122

SARDINE BONE BROTH:.. 123

TURMERIC PASTE AKA GOLDEN PASTE 124

VEGGIE MIX... 126

FERMENTED VEGETABLES.. 128

DIY YOGURT.. 132

MY FINAL THOUGHTS ON RAW FEEDING.................................... 137

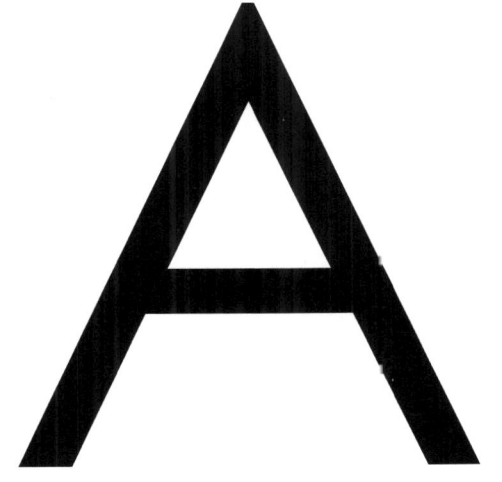

A - An Introduction to Raw Feeding

My name is Kimberly, I have four dogs, and I'm a raw feeder.

In 2013, I worked with a local raw food company to transition my dogs to a raw food diet. I was nervous about the cost, and I didn't understand anything about dog nutrition. I knew my dog, Rodrigo, was suffering from a myriad of health issues because of dry dog food and I prayed raw feeding was the answer.

Today, more than nine years later, Rodrigo is a healthy twelve-year-old senior dog. We always joke we should waltz Rodrigo down to the vet clinic where his first vet predicted our dog would need to be euthanized at three years of age. It would be worth the trip if we could change the vet's mind about raw feeding. He'd probably have us arrested for trespassing.

REBOOTING A NOVICE'S GUIDE

When speaking to pet parents new to raw feeding, I always say learning about feeding a fresh food diet "is a marathon, not a sprint." We're constantly learning from our dogs, fellow pet parents, veterinarians, and other leaders in this amazing community. Over the past several years, I've changed how I feed my dogs and decided to update this book because raw feeding is easier than I shared the first time!

I wrote and published my first A to Z series in April 2014 on my blog, Keep the Tail Wagging®. In this book, A Novice's Guide to Raw Feeding, you will find a guide to transitioning to raw feeding and information about raw feeding using the alphabet as a guide.

When I started down this road, I thought raw feeding was too expensive; today, I buy 99% of my supplies through a local raw food co-op, which cut my monthly budget by more than 50%. When I started, I thought raw feeding was too complicated; today, I find raw feeding easier than feeding kibble.

4

I wrote this book to help animal lovers. Keep in mind that this book is based on my experience with my dogs; one experience in a sea of many. Enjoy.

WHY I FEED MY DOGS RAW DOG FOOD

When I switched to raw, it gave Rodrigo relief from environmental allergies, food allergies, ear infections, chronic diarrhea, skin rashes, itchy paws, and joint pain. Today, I understand we feed raw because it's biologically appropriate. A high-carb diet filled with overly processed foods contributed to my dog's health issues.

During the first two weeks of feeding raw, we saw a huge improvement in Rodrigo's health. At the time, I fed our dogs raw in the morning and kibble during the evening as we transitioned slowly over three months. The addition of fresh foods to a diet of processed foods made a significant difference.

I transitioned my dogs slowly because I was concerned about the cost of feeding raw and my dog's sensitive gut. We tried mixing raw and kibble together and learned quickly this was too much for Rodrigo's gut as the two diets battled it out (they have different pH levels).

Rodrigo, Sydney, and Blue were transitioned in 2013. I've transitioned three more dogs to raw, Scout, Zoey, and Apollo, and I chose an immediate transition (cold turkey), and they took to the diet without issue.

WHY I WRITE ABOUT RAW FEEDING

I write about raw feeding to share what I've learned with others so more people can experience the amazing transformation in their dogs and possibly defy a veterinarian's diagnosis.

When I became a raw feeder and started researching dog nutrition, I found it complicated, contradictory, and overwhelming. One person told me yogurt was great for dogs; another person told me yogurt is bad for dogs. Some raw feeding groups welcome all models of raw feeding, while others ban the mention of vegetables. And then there are the folks who are hyper focused on balance, so much so they've soaked all the fun out of raw feeding.

I write about raw feeding because the raw feeding community is all many pet lovers have, and I feel we should all share our experiences and this is my way to pay forward the time others have taken to share their experiences and knowledge with me.

TRANSITIONING A DOG TO A RAW FOOD DIET

There are many paths to take for people who want to transition their dog to raw dog food; below is what I recommend based on my experience with my dogs and what I've learned over the past nine years from other raw feeders and leaders in our community.

START EDUCATING YOURSELF ABOUT RAW FEEDING

The most important step is to start educating yourself about raw feeding. Join raw feeding groups, watch YouTube videos, connect with a pro-raw veterinarian and local raw feeders, and pick up a few books. Don't allow your education to come from one place because many of us are self-taught, and what works for my dogs may not work for your dogs. Instead, soak up as much knowledge from as many sources as possible so you're prepared to meet your dogs' needs.

START WITH A QUALITY PREMADE RAW BRAND

Over the years we've seen a sharp uptick in raw feeding brands, but this increase in options doesn't make choosing a brand easy. If you're looking for a raw food brand that is a good fit for your dog, head to your local independent pet store and ask the manager/owner for recommendations.

This is the easiest way to transition because the sourcing and balancing are taken care of for you. Of course, you'll pay for amazing service too.

If your budget is tight, joining a raw food co-op and sourcing from hunters, farmers, and people looking to clean out their freezers is an option.

The following are brands I feed to my dogs.

- Solutions Pet Products
- Darwin's Natural Pet Food
- Wild Coast Raw
- Natural Pet Pantry
- Columbia River Pet Food
- GreenTripe.com

There are many options available today. You can buy premade raw online, at your local pet store, or through a raw food co-op (Visit KeepTheTailWagging.com/coop for a current list).

Although premade raw can be expensive, it allows pet parents to quickly transition their dogs to a balanced raw diet while giving them time to research recipes, sourcing, storage, and budget.

LOOK FOR SOURCING IN YOUR AREA

If your budget is tight, then consider DIY raw feeding. I transitioned to DIY a year after I started feeding raw. It's more affordable and appeases the control freak in me since I choose the ingredients and can adjust on the fly.

To get started, you'll need to find sourcing in your area, which may include:

Look for a meat supplier, butcher, farmer, or hunter in your area; make sure your local laws allow you to buy from hunters (this isn't legal in every state).

Look to see if there is a raw food co-op in your area; this is a group of people who buy in bulk together at discounted prices.

Check prices and connect with the meat manager at your local grocery store and Ethnic markets.

Look to see if there is a Farmer's Market in your area for fresh meat and vegetables.

Once you secure sourcing that meets your budget and will create a healthy meal, you can move on to transitioning your dog to raw feeding.

TRANSITION YOUR DOG TO RAW

One mistake I made was to introduce my dogs to too many proteins and other ingredients too soon. It resulted in diarrhea for two days and I ran back to kibble with my tail between my legs.

I also made a call to a local raw food company.

If you're working with a healthy dog or puppy, you can transition as slowly or as quickly as you want. There's mixed information when it comes to "balance" and although I still say "I don't balance my own diet," I've changed my mind when it comes to my dogs. I believe in balance over time (more on this later) for adult dogs.

However, puppies are different.

Because puppies are growing quickly, don't have fat to store vitamins, and have trouble regulating nutrients it's essential their diet is balanced daily. So, I, but when I'm feeding a puppy, I feed commercial raw and I work with a meal formulator to make sure my DIY diet is on point.

That being said, there are five ways I recommend transitioning to raw:

1 – HYBRID DIET AND PREMADE (OR DIY)

A hybrid diet is splitting the meals between raw and kibble; this is how I started. I fed commercial raw in the morning and kibble in the evening until we ran out of kibble. This allowed me to take my time, it took away any worry about balance, and it was more affordable than transitioning straight away.

Mixing raw and kibble together was fine for two of our dogs, but the combination made Rodrigo sick and we never did it again. Since then, I learned some dogs do get sick if fed raw meat and kibble in the same meal because...

Some feel raw and kibble digest at different rates with kibble taking longer to digest, holding the raw meat in the gut longer.

Some feel raw creates an acidic gut and kibble creates a more alkaline gut and the two don't mix well.

2 – PREMADE (COMMERCIAL) RAW

As I stated earlier, commercial raw is convenient. If you buy from a quality brand, you don't have to worry about balance, sourcing, or the ingredients. Another benefit of commercial raw is it allows you to add variety to the diet and it gives you a break when you need it.

3 – DIY WITH A BASE MIX

If you want to feed a balanced diet but you're not interested in spreadsheets, calculators, science books, and software, look for a base mix that doesn't have white potatoes or other unnecessary grains. I began using a base mix several years ago - it's easy, and it's hitting all the nutritional marks.

Using a base mix is less expensive than feeding commercial raw, making DIY easy. I start with 80/10/10 (80% muscle meat, 10% bone, and 10% organ meat). For every quart (or 10-11 lbs.) of raw, I mix ¼ cup to 1 cup of the base mix. It's that easy. More on this later.

When it comes to feeding puppies, I prefer premade raw (or DIY formulated by a professional) over base mix to ensure I'm hitting all of the nutritional marks.

COURSES IN RAW FEEDING

If you're nervous about DIY, take a course or workshop.

-   **Feed Real Movement** – a membership comes with monthly nutritional consults. And Feed Real offers online and local raw feeding workshops.

-   Raw Feeding 101 – Scott Marshall, the founder of Raw Feeding 101, offers a course, bootcamp, and meal formulation services.

4 – WORK WITH A MEAL FORMULATOR

Working with a meal formulator allows you to feed your puppy or dog DIY, saving you money over time. A professional meal formulator will customize your dog's raw food diet based on age, size, and activity level while keeping your sourcing and budget in mind.

You may be able to find recipes available and some of these are fine (in rotation) for adult dogs. I would be hesitant to trust a stranger's recipe for my puppy or dog.

WHAT TO FEED A DOG

I feed my dogs a variety of proteins without going overboard. I start with 80% muscle meat, 10% bone, and 10% organ meat, adding a base mix (Dr. Harvey's Raw Vibrance and Paradigm) for balance.

I also feed my dogs:

- Pasture-raised chicken eggs *
- Sardines (raw, canned with olive oil, canned with water & no salt added)
- Mackerel (raw)
- Salmon (cooked)**
- Canned or baked oysters
- Bone broth
- Kefir
- Raw goat's milk
- Homemade yogurt

*Feeding poached eggs cooked the egg whites enough to deactivate the properties that block biotin while keeping the yolk raw-ish. I've also fed eggs sunny-side up.

**There is a risk of salmon poisoning on the west coast for dogs fed raw salmon or steelhead trout from the Pacific ocean. To be on the safe side, I cook their salmon and trout before feeding to my dogs.

HOW MUCH RAW TO FEED A DOG

Many raw food calculators online take your dog's weight and activity level and tell you how much you should feed your dog daily. I weigh my dogs' meals to avoid overfeeding them (a past bad habit of mine). A general guideline is:

Feed 2% of a dog's body weight to help them lose weight or for low-activity dogs.

Feed 2.5% of a dog's body weight to help them maintain weight.

Feed 3% or more of a dog's body weight for active dogs.

I used an online raw food calculator for each of my dogs, and monitored each dog's weight over several weeks, adjusting how much I fed until their weight stabilized. It was a lot easier (and faster) than I explained.

I also adjust my dogs' diet based on the time of the year. For instance, my dogs eat less in the winter when it's too cold for long walks.

MONITOR YOUR DOG'S STOOL

This step never goes away. I learn a lot when I clean the yard.

- I know when I've fed too much bone (or not enough).
- I know when someone is having tummy troubles.
- I know when a protein is or isn't working for one of my dogs.
- I know how long protein digestion takes compared to plant-based meals (48 hours vs. 24 hours).

LEARNING FROM MY DOG'S STOOL

What I want to see are small, solid poops. However, this isn't always the case. The following are what I see with my dogs and how I adjust their diet.

White, Hard Poop: too much calcium or insufficient organ meat; increase organ meat or decrease bone.

Soft Poop: too much organ meat or not enough bone; add more raw meaty bones.

Soft Poop: reaction to a new protein; solve with fiber (supplement or fur), organic pumpkin, organic sweet potatoes, or slippery elm.

Soft Poop: protein intolerance: stop feeding the protein.

These are just a few examples. As you become familiar with your dog's poop, you'll be able to identify what's happening and make quick adjustments.

LET YOUR DOG TELL YOU WHAT TO FEED

You may find there are proteins your dog loves and others your dog turns away from; this is okay. Alternating proteins weekly or on another steady schedule will keep your dog engaged while allowing you to determine which foods do and do not work for your dog.

Sometimes, your dog won't eat at all (or won't eat all of their meal). With my dogs, I've learned this is perfectly okay if it happens and there are no signs of illness. Sometimes a dog will self-fast. And our oldest dog eats less food.

HOW MANY TIMES OF DAY TO FEED A DOG

There are several ways to feed a dog. I've fed puppies three times a day, transitioning to two times a day at six months. Our adult dogs are fed twice daily, and I fast them once or twice a week.

Feeding Once a Day: Feeding a dog once a day eliminates the need to have a "fasting" day. Our dogs have a 24-hour fast between meals. This is for adult dogs only; puppies require multiple meals a day.

Feeding Twice a Day: This seems to be most common when feeding dogs. I used to feed my dogs at 12-hour intervals. Today, I feed my dogs between 9 am and 5 pm, equating to a 16-hour fast each day.

Feeding Multiple Times a Day: This works best for puppies and small dogs.

Benefits of Fasting: I was introduced to fasting by a human nutritionist and other raw feeders. I saw some raw feeders fasted their dogs on a schedule, while others fasted by feeding once daily.

13

Fasting allows the gut to take a break from constantly digesting food. It allows the body to heal itself, which is why fasting is recommended when a dog has diarrhea. And fasting increases microphage levels to destroy harmful bacteria, viruses, and toxins.

Fasting may seem cruel, but fasting is a natural process that even humans do on occasion. My dogs self-fast when they have an upset tummy; I only get concerned if the fast continues more than 48 hours. At that time, I call our vet.

Never fast puppies as they need all of their nutrient to help their rapidly maturing bodies. If a dog is sick, consult with your veterinarian before fasting your dog. And, if your dog is rapidly losing weight due to a fasting schedule, PLEASE PLEASE PLEASE do not continue. There are pet parents who have been pressured into an intense fasting regimen to the detriment of the dog.

SOME DOGS GO THROUGH A DETOX

Some dogs experience a detox period after switching to raw food. Dog owners share their dogs…

- start shedding a lot
- have mucus-covered stool
- eye boogers
- smelly ears
- have dry skin

…and other mild symptoms that make them nervous about raw.

Before freaking out and racing to the vet, ask yourself if your dog's behavior has changed (are they acting sick?) and double-check the symptoms of detox others have reported. They tend to last a few days to a couple of weeks.

While this may be unnerving, a detox period is the system's way of ridding excess toxins and other unhealthy things after being on a kibble diet.

And then again, some people don't believe in detox, and some dogs don't experience detox. Mine didn't detox.

ADDING SUPPLEMENTS TO A RAW DIET FOR DOGS

When you initially transition a dog to a raw food diet, I don't think adding supplements is a great idea. You may be tempted to add things other raw feeders tell you about, but it'll quickly become expensive. Plus, strangers on social media mean well, but they don't know anything about you or your dog (health, diet, budget, etc.), and their recommendations may not work for your dog.

My dogs no longer needed certain supplements (joint supplement, digestive supplement, fish oil) once I transitioned to raw because their diet covered these needs.

I've saved money by taking a conservative stance on supplements and only giving my dogs what they need.

My last bit of advice on the supplements is to go with quality, proven brands. Not every human supplement is suitable for dogs.

Now, Let's dive a bit deeper into raw feeding.

DEFINITION OF RAW FEEDING

Raw feeding is a diet that consists of a ratio of raw muscle meat, organ meat, and bone. Raw feeders believe feeding a diet of raw dog food is species-appropriate, meaning the diet is what dogs are meant to eat. We know dogs have evolved from the Grey Wolf and raw feeding attempts to mimic a wolf's diet while considering the sourcing of ingredients and how dogs have adapted over the centuries.

One reason we prefer raw feeding to kibble is raw feeding has a long history. Many people don't know kibble hasn't been around for very long. It was invented during World War II as a solution when aluminum (initially used for canned dog food) was redirected to the war efforts. Pet food manufacturers had to think of something new for their customers. And that's why we have kibble.

Over the years, pet food manufacturers have found they can make more money by using inferior ingredients (corn and other grains, meat byproducts, cheap synthetic vitamins), call their food balanced, and when dogs got sick, they'd sell pet parents "prescription" food that acted as a bandage instead of a cure for health issues.

While pet food manufacturers keep our dogs sick with their food, raw feeding is curing many illnesses. Dogs live longer, healthier lives when raw feeding is combined with a healthy weight, regular exercise, minimal vaccinations, and limited exposure to flea and tick chemicals and other toxins.

Ingredients in a raw food diet consist of approximately 80% raw muscle meat, 10% raw bone, 5% liver, and 5% offal (secreting organs like the pancreas, spleen, testicles, ovaries, and kidneys). While this is where many raw feeders start, it becomes clear this is not a diet that can meet a dog's nutritional needs and adjust as necessary.

RAW FEEDING MODELS (DIETS)

While everyone ultimately ends up feeding what is best for their dog, we all start from one of two main models of raw feeding: BARF and PREY Model.

BARF MODEL OF RAW FEEDING

The BARF model of raw feeding is the most common and what we see in most premade raw brands. BARF is an acronym for Biologically Appropriate Raw Food. The BARF model of raw feeding consists of raw muscle meat, raw bone, raw organ meat, raw fruits and vegetables, and other natural supplements.

Proponents of the BARF model of raw feeding believe all ingredients in a natural BARF diet meet the dietary/nutritional needs for our dogs.

Critics of the BARF model of raw feeding believe adding produce is unnecessary and serves as a filler or, possibly, fiber. Some think dogs aren't capable of breaking down a diet heavy in fruits and vegetables due to the cellulose wall, which acts as a barrier, preventing dogs from being able to access the nutrients. Breaking down the vegetables in a dog's system places stress on the pancreas and can lead to pancreatitis.

Although the BARF model can be fed whole, we often see it fed as a ground diet to dogs.

The ingredients in the BARF model of raw feeding call for a reduction of the muscle meat to account for the fruits and vegetables: 65%-75% muscle meat instead of 80%, 10% raw bone, 5% liver, and 5% offal (secreting organs like pancreas, spleen, testicles, ovaries, and kidneys).

PREY MODEL OF RAW FEEDING

The PREY model of raw feeding leans towards feeding the whole animal and focuses on food sources for supplements; for example, if your dog needs a joint supplement, feed him cuts of meat high in chondroitin and glucosamine (e.g., duck feet).

While Prey model raw feeding seems to follow a wolf's diet more closely than the BARF model, PMR (prey model raw) followers do add supplements when necessary. They may use vegetables for weight loss and herbs for medicinal purposes.

There is also a question of whether wolves eat the stomach contents of their vegetarian prey. Some believe wolves shake out the stomach contents, only eating the meat, while others believe wolves eat the whole animal, including the animal's last vegetarian meal.

This "stomach contents" theory is based on a 40-year study by L. David Mech, who lived with and observed wolves, documenting his findings in two books:

- Wolves on the Hunt
- Wolves' Behavior and Ecology

The ingredients in the Prey model of raw feeding are 80% muscle meat, 10% raw bone, 5% liver, and 5% offal (secreting organs like the pancreas, spleen, testicles, ovaries, and kidneys).

Other raw feeding models include NRC (or Science-Based), Rotational Mono Feeding (RMF), and a modified version of a model.

WHY KIBBLE ISN'T GOOD FOR DOGS (OR CATS)

Kibble is an over-processed, repeatedly baked food that has lost all nutritional value, so brands add in a bucket load of synthetic vitamins from a purchased bought in a mix, preservatives to allow the food to sit in a warehouse for months on end, and a chemical based "natural flavor" to make the food appeal to dogs.

Kibble lacks moisture, leading to a constant state of dehydration and digestive issues. Because the digestive system is closely tied to the immune system, a kibble diet will leave some dogs with poor health, like my Rodrigo, or worse.

THE MEAT AS THE FIRST INGREDIENT MYTH

We've been told to look for meat as the first ingredient, but this isn't a sign of a "quality" kibble. For instance, one of the leading kibble brands offers the following on their first line of ingredients: Deboned Chicken, Chicken

Meal (source of Glucosamine), Turkey Meal, Peas, Pea Protein, and Chicken Fat (preserved with Mixed Tocopherols).

The deboned chicken has water, and water adds weight. "deboned chicken" is first because of the water, not the chicken.

Chicken meal is chicken with the water removed, but in this food, they use the meal as a source of glucosamine because it is mostly chicken bone and cartilage, not chicken meat.

Turkey meal is the THIRD ingredient, meaning there is more water (deboned chicken) and bone (chicken meal) than turkey in this food.

The brand adds peas and pea protein to boost the protein amount.

Chicken fat causes the kibble to go bad faster; once the bag is opened, the fat begins to oxidize. And guess what! Transferring the food to a plastic container will make it go bad even faster; the dog food bags are made from products that slow oxidation, but plastic containers are not.

It's all a crock.

People need real, whole, minimally processed foods to thrive. As humans, if making healthy eating choices has improved our health, it shouldn't be a leap to realize this same logic applies to their cats and dogs.

Our dogs are meant to eat a diet of raw muscle meat, bone, and organs, despite what the traditional veterinarian community and the big pet food companies are trying to tell us. What did dogs eat before commercial can and dry dog food hit store shelves? They ate what we ate along with a diet of raw meat, a diet high in vitamins, minerals, antioxidants, healthy fats, living enzymes, and moisture.

As people, we're told eating fewer processed foods, whole foods, and foods free of chemicals and additives are better for us; is it so hard to believe the same is true for our dogs?

After saying everything to this point, I must add, for some people, kibble is the only option. If I had to feed kibble to my dogs, I would add as much fresh food as I could afford to their diet, including:

- Cooked lean meat
- Canned sardines
- Canned oysters (not smoked)
- Poached eggs
- Broccoli
- Green beans
- Apples
- Berries

COMMON FEARS ABOUT RAW FEEDING

Many veterinarians aren't fans of raw feeding. They are concerned about our ability to meet our dogs' nutritional needs in a homemade diet, among other valid concerns.

However, raw feeding isn't the dangerous diet many would have us believe.

IS RAW FEEDING SAFE?

Absolutely! Yes, handling raw meat does expose our dogs and us to bacteria. However, proper food handling and hygiene practices are all we need to stay safe. Raw feeding is still an option if an inspiring raw feeder or a dog has a compromised immune system. Many premade raw brands make packaging that reduces exposure to raw meat when feeding our dogs, or you can feed HPP brands.

High-Pressure Pasteurization (HPP): HPP is a process that reduces pathogens in raw meat. Some people believe HPP destroys many nutrients in raw; I can't entirely agree because the process has come a long way over the years. Plus, it makes raw more accessible to dog owners concerned about the bacteria in a raw diet.

WILL THE BACTERIA IN RAW MAKE MY DOG SICK?

Nope! Unless your dog has a compromised immune system, raw is perfectly safe. A dog's system has several defenses against the bacteria in raw. Their saliva has properties that kill bacteria, their gut isn't very hospitable to bacteria, and their digestive tract is short and processes food quickly and efficiently.

If you are raising a dog with a compromised immune system, speak with a holistic vet who is experienced in raw feeding before crossing the diet off your list. A home-cooked diet may be best for your dog if raw isn't an option.

Our dog, Scout, lived with cancer for more than 18 months; he was fed a raw food diet the entire time and he thrived.

IS RAW DOG FOOD BALANCED?

Yes! A quality commercial brand offers balanced recipes; some offer recipes that allow pet parents to add whole foods or supplements that help achieve balance. And it's easier for pet parents to balance a DIY diet – we are learning through courses, through software (Animal Diet Formulator), and by working with meal formulators.

IS RAW FEEDING EXPENSIVE?

I would love to say, "No, raw feeding is cheaper than feeding kibble." It depends on where you live, the resources available, and how much time you can commit to the diet.

For instance, I spend more than 50% less money learning how to make a balanced raw meal for my dogs than when I bought premade raw.

I feed a combination of DIY and premade raw, buying 99% of the food through a local raw food co-op, from local farms and homesteaders, and freezer dumps (free).

A raw food co-op is an organization that orders raw from meat suppliers, local farms, and pet food distributors at wholesale prices. There is an annual membership fee, order frequency, and pick-up dates. Co-ops are not the same as a raw food brand that delivers to your door.

Visit my blog to search for a raw food co-op in your area: KeepTheTailWagging.com/COOP

DO RAW FEEDERS MISTRUST VETERINARIANS?

Yes, and no. The first veterinarian who saw my puppies, Rodrigo and Sydney, was intolerant of questions, didn't like rescue dogs, and would not have been supportive of a raw food diet. In my experience, while many veterinarians don't support raw, they may get on board if you're able to demonstrate that you will do the research needed to learn how to feed your dog a nutritionally complete, raw diet.

I respect a veterinarian's education and experience. I am fortunate to work with an integrative veterinarian who supports my choice to feed raw.

FINDING THE RIGHT RAW FOOD SOURCES

When I'm looking into a new source, I'm interested in the following:

- Where does the meat come from?

- Is it 3D or 4D (diseased, dying, down, or dead) meat?
- What was the animal fed? Grass? Grain?
- Was the animal ethically raised?
- Was the animal subjected to hormones, antibiotics, or other chemicals?
- What is the cost? Per pound?
- If it's a premade raw brand, I'm also interested in knowing the following:
- What are the ingredients?
- Is the blend nutritionally complete?
- Does the food contain synthetic vitamins? If so, how much?
- What percentage of the food is vegetation?
- Does the brand use high-pressure pasteurization?

There are many options out there, and the answers to these questions help me make the right choices for my dogs. For me, the only deal breakers are the 3D/4D meat and chemicals.

SYNTHETIC VITAMINS

If a brand is using a few synthetic vitamins, I won't write off their food as long as it's a brand I trust. Sometimes, a brand will use synthetic vitamins because whole food isn't available (or isn't available consistently), or the whole food options increase the cost.

If a brand is heavily leaning on synthetic vitamins, then I'll pass because I worry about the long-term impact synthetic vitamins can have on our dogs. Synthetic vitamins are less bioavailable and can be harder to digest; especially with our senior dogs. And, if someone is using a vitamin mix, I worry the sourcing may not be as high quality and can also lead to health issues over time.

HIGH-PRESSURE PASTEURIZATION

While HPP food isn't my favorite, I don't mind feeding it to my dogs. I'm not a fan of the texture; I prefer raw dog food that looks like my DIY – you can see the meat, the vegetables, etc. (I add oysters). But, if we're talking about a respected brand that uses HPP, if I score a free (or discounted) case of their food, I'm taking it proudly and feeding the food to my dogs.

VEGETABLES

Many raw food brands follow the BARF model will add up to 25% vegetation to their recipe. This seems like too much (for my dogs). I don't mind adding this food in rotation with other foods. It's just not my favorite.

B - Balance, Bacteria, Behavior, and Raw Dog Food

BALANCING A RAW FOOD DIET

One of the critiques raw feeders receive is our diet isn't balanced. And there is a reason for concern. When I wrote the first version of this book, I shared that I balance over time for my adult dogs. This hasn't changed – I still balance over time, but I also…

- use meal formulation software
- use a base mix
- occasionally nutrient test my dogs
- ask a trusted meal formulator to review my recipes

I sincerely believe no one knows what "balance" is for our dogs. Many people have a piece of the puzzle, but every dog is different. I have a dog that absorbs nutrients differently than the others because of a health condition. What's balanced for him may not always be balanced for the others, which is why it's a good idea to have dogs nutrient tested.

DETERMINING IF YOUR RAW FED DOG IS HEALTHY

I see a lot of new raw feeders panicking because their dog has diarrhea after the first couple of meals of raw. This can happen, but I won't tell you not to go to the vet if you're concerned.

When I fed my dogs their first raw meal – it wasn't Darwin's Pet, it was a random recipe someone shared with me – they had insane diarrhea the next day. That meal cost a lot of money with all the ingredients; it was too rich for my dogs. So, I understand the concern.

Diarrhea for a day or two doesn't worry me unless it's accompanied by other signs my dog is sick.

We often want someone else to tell us to go to the vet because we don't want to believe our pets are sick, but it's not a good idea to trust strangers on social media.

You know your dog. Even if you got your dog a week ago, if your dog looks and behaves sick, please call your veterinarian.

BACTERIA IN RAW DOG FOOD

Many people are worried the bacteria in raw meat will make their dogs or their human family members sick. If you've made a turkey dinner for your family and no one got sick, then you can handle feeding raw to your dog. The same meat handling rules apply – wash your hands, wash the dishes, wash the utensils, wash the surfaces.

I wash my hands after doing meal prep, I clean the kitchen, and I wash my dogs' dishes daily.

Dogs are designed to consume raw meat because it's species-appropriate:

the saliva of dogs kills bacteria with each bite because it contains an enzyme called lysozyme that kills harmful bacteria.

a dog's digestive system is shorter and pushes through the food fast enough to prevent any surviving bacteria from setting up camp, but not so fast that our dogs' systems won't absorb the nutrients they need to be happy and healthy.

And for those who warn us that dogs will shed salmonella, remind them of all the dry dog food recalls due to salmonella. Let them know dogs can also be exposed to salmonella...

- in standing water
- in dog poop
- in bird droppings
- in rodents

- in reptiles
- in grass

BEHAVIOR OF RAW FED DOGS

In the years since I wrote the first version of my book, I've come to take more ownership over my dogs' behavior. I partly blamed my dog's diet (dry dog food) for his behavior. While the blood-sugar spikes of a high carb diet weren't doing him any favors, they weren't all to blame.

The problem with high-carb dry dog food is it's like me drinking a 16-ounce Mountain Dew before bedtime. Our dogs start exhibiting behavioral challenges, have a hard time focusing, and we wonder what's going on.

I've met a lot of dog trainers who incorporate a discussion on nutrition when working with clients. It's not an attempt to push raw feeding on someone; these trainers are more focused on recommending more fresh food be added to the bowl.

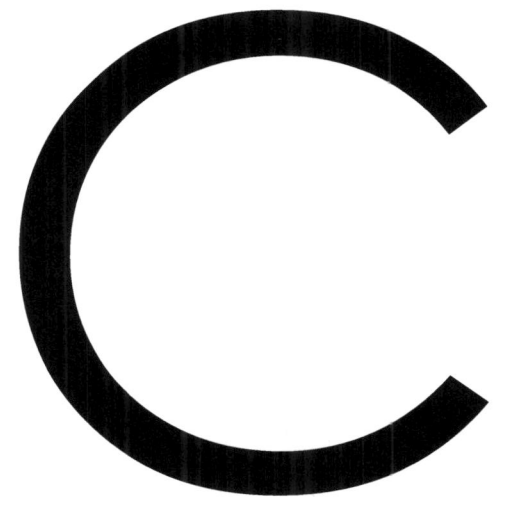

C - Cost, Calcium, Carnivores, and Raw Dog Food

COST OF RAW FEEDING

In the first version of this book, I was spending $200-$250/month on dog food, treats, supplements, toys, and other supplies for four dogs. The only change is I now have senior dogs in the house, and the cost of raising senior dogs is a little higher in some areas (pet insurance, veterinarian care, and supplementation).

I've even scored a few new connections:

- I made friends with several people in the meat department of my local grocery store, and they give me a heads up on overstock discounts.

- The man who slaughters the area's farm animals is a friend of mine and saves precious organs for me when he can.

- Several of my friends are homesteaders or partners in a cow or pig; they give me the parts they don't keep. They also give me old meat and bones when they clear their freezers.

- And I have a few friends who own freeze-driers!!!

I have pet insurance for my dogs, which I can't recommend enough. We've had two cancer dogs (yes, raw fed dogs can develop cancer) in our home, and pet insurance covered 90% of the cost.

You may have read raw feeding costs less than feeding kibble. However, this isn't the case for everyone. For many raw feeders, the savings are seen with fewer visits to the veterinarian and fewer prescription medications.

10 WAYS TO DECREASE COSTS

The following are a few ideas to cut costs of raw feeding.

1. Shop through a local raw food co-op; find more here: KeepTheTailWagging.com/coop.

2. Order ingredients/products in bulk.

3. Shop at pet stores that have sales on fresh pet food (raw, cooked, dehydrated, freeze-dried). Ask about frequent buyer discounts.

4. Get to know your grocery store's meat/seafood manager and asked to be notified of upcoming sales; keep an eye on meat that is close to expiring – these are a great source for DIY dog treats.

5. Shop at discount, outlet, and Ethnic grocery stores. You'll find a lot of variety and cool options for your dog's next meal.

6. Buy pasture-raised chicken, duck, and quail eggs from friends and neighbors.

7. Make your own veggie mix, bone broth, golden paste, yogurt, kefir, and dog treats. A food dehydrator and pressure cooker are great tools to have.

8. Look for a restaurant supply store in your area – US Foods has stores around the country.

9. Connect with friends who fish or hunt; they may be willing to share or sell what they can't store.

10. Subscribe to the mailing list of your favorite brands to be notified about sales; and save money in anticipation of Black Friday / Cyber Monday sales.

CALCIUM IN RAW DOG FOOD

My dogs get calcium through their diet, primarily through ground bone. I used to feed green tripe as a backup because green tripe offers a 1:1 calcium to phosphorous ratio. However, green tripe doesn't offer enough calcium for it to be a viable substitute for bone.

I don't use bone meal in my meal prep because I read most food-grade bone meal on the market is heat processed, making it difficult for dogs to digest. I'm also concerned about sourcing. When I was looking for quality bone meals, I couldn't find any sourced in the US.

And despite the name, bone broth isn't a bone substitute.

ARE DOGS CARNIVORES OR OMNIVORES?

Some people believe dogs are omnivores, while others believe dogs are carnivores. I fall into the carnivore category because of their teeth (made for ripping meat from the bone and chomping bone) and what I believe to be a species-appropriate diet that includes raw meat, raw bone, and raw offal/organ meat.

My opinion isn't based on science or studying wolves and dogs; it's based on my experience as a raw feeder. Therefore, I may be wrong, and I'm okay with being wrong. But I don't think I am. But I could be.

There is also a disagreement in the raw feeding community about whether dogs need fruits and vegetables. Here are my thoughts.

I believe wolves and wild dogs do eat fruits and vegetables; they forage between hunts.

I think wolves and wild dogs take from nature what they need, and fruits and vegetables can be medicinal or a snack.

I think some wolves and wild dogs shake out the stomach content of their vegetarian prey to get rid of the vegetation, while others eat the stomach contents.

I believe dogs (at least my dogs) can consume vegetables without taxing their pancreas because I freeze, puree, or blanche (cook for a few minutes in boiling water) to break the cellular wall before feeding it to my dogs. Feeding a BARF diet will not cause my dogs to have pancreatitis.

Not all fruits and vegetables lead to a blood sugar spike; I choose low glycemic vegetables because they are a great source of fiber and add additional nutrients to the bowl.

I feed raw raspberries, blueberries, blackberries, strawberries, apples, and pears to my dogs as a treat when they're in season. I don't feed bananas because not everyone is a fan.

Feeding my dogs organic vegetables and fruit doesn't make them omnivores; it just makes them well-fed carnivores.

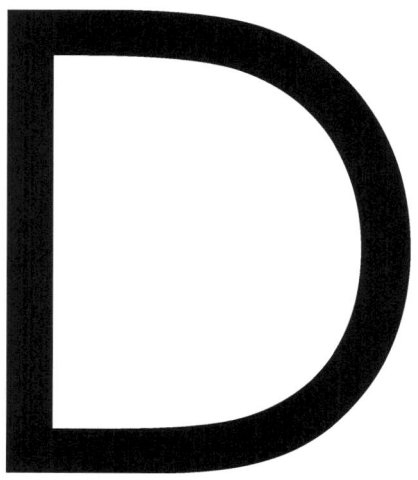

D - Disease, Dehydrated Food, Dog Dishes, and Dog Treats for Raw Fed Dogs

DISEASES CURED BY RAW FEEDING

I'm not a veterinarian, so I'm not going to pretend I know how to treat diseases in dogs. What I do know is there are health issues that are improved or cured when dogs are fed a species-appropriate diet.

Understanding Rodrigo's gut issues taught me the gut is closely connected to the immune system. When Rodrigo's gut wasn't healthy, he had:

- Daily loose stool, diarrhea, and gas
- Chronic ear infections
- Angry, red rashes on his back and tummy
- Itchy paws he licked until sores developed
- Environmental and food allergies
- Increased inflammation and joint pain

Over the years, a combination of a species-appropriate diet, adding fiber, and feeding the right proteins has helped strengthen Rodrigo's gut, which has, in turn, strengthened his immune system.

Rodrigo hasn't had ear infections or rashes since I switched him to raw in 2013. He's stopped obsessively licking his paws shortly after being switched to raw dog food. And his poop is solid and small.

A few diseases can be improved with a raw diet, including:

Diabetes: a raw food diet doesn't cause blood sugar spikes like kibble, which is higher in carb content. If you choose to feed BARF, you can select the lower glycemic vegetables and fruit if you're watching for blood sugar spikes.

Pancreatitis: the living enzymes in a raw food diet reduce the stress on the pancreas by sharing the job of providing enzymes to break down the food.

Kidney Disease: I've read repeatedly dry dog food is the worst thing you can feed a dog with kidney disease; it's often made with inferior proteins, taxing on the kidneys because of all the synthetic ingredients, and it's dehydrating. On the other hand, a fresh food diet is ideal for a dog with kidney failure because you can control the quality of the protein you feed, a raw food diet is moisture-rich, and there are no harsh/ mystery ingredients.

Reducing protein isn't necessary for all animals with kidney disease; I recommend finding a holistic vet experienced in raw feeding who can help you build the right, species-appropriate diet.

Joint Health: a raw food diet doesn't incur inflammation in the body, reducing joint pain.

Obesity: feeding our dogs lean meats, healthy animal fats, and organic greens will lead to a healthier metabolism and immune system — which leads to a healthier weight.

Dental Health: Kibble doesn't clean our dog's teeth. Our dogs don't chew long enough for any teeth cleaning to happen, and I have a $700 teeth cleaning bill to show you they don't clean a cat's teeth either. What does clean my dogs' teeth is chewing on raw meaty bones and recreational bones; I brush my cat's teeth.

If your dog has an illness or disease, please speak with a holistic veterinarian experienced in raw and home-cooked diets for dogs to learn what you should feed your dog to help improve his/her health.

DEHYDRATED VS. FREEZE-DRIED DOG FOOD

When food is dehydrated, the heat evaporates the water from the ingredients. Although its low heat, it allows many of the nutrients to remain intact, the food is still being cooked, and the cellular structure of the food is being altered.

With freeze-dried dog food, the food is frozen, then placed in a vacuum chamber where the ice is evaporated. The temperature remains below freezing, and the nutrients remain intact

Dehydrated and freeze-dried dog food are great as food toppers, convenient to feed when traveling, and an alternative for people who aren't ready (or able) to feed their dogs a raw food diet. I feed my cat freeze-dried cat food – he loves it.

DOG DISHES FOR RAW FED DOGS

When one of my dogs was diagnosed with cancer, she went from being highly food motivated to refusing to eat. In a panic, I contacted a friend who recommended feeding her from a flat surface. It worked and I began feeding all of my dogs from flat dishes.

Feeding from a flat surface (pasta dishes, plates, divider trays) has been a game changer for my dogs.

- The smell of the food isn't overwhelming.
- I can spread the foods out, allowing my dogs to choose what they want to eat (they usually go for the duck feet, wings, or quail first).
- Allowing this choice increases engagement at meal times.
- My picky eater is less choosy.
- The dogs can reach all of their food easily without pressing their noses in the corners of the dish.
- There is less of a risk of whisker fatigue (something mostly seen in cats).
- Their vision isn't blocked by the sides of a dog dish.

DOG TREATS FOR RAW FED DOGS

Once I began paying attention to the ingredients in my dogs' food, it didn't take long for me to become obsessed with their treats. After learning about the pet food industry and reading the ingredients panel of many treats, I settled on single ingredient protein treats. However, quality protein treats are expensive - $15 a bag or more.

For $15, I can make several bags of treats with a dehydrator and meat from:

Local homesteaders who are giving away organ meat. • Discounted meat at grocery stores and outlet markets

Freezer dumps (found through friends).

I updated to a LEM food dehydrator and I love it. It's easy to use, has a tray at the bottom to catch any fat I missed when trimming the meat, and it has a timer to avoid overcooking the treats.

For more variety, I'm also a Real Dog Box subscriber and receive a treat box filled with healthy, single ingredient treats and chews for less than 50% of the cost in stores.

E - Eggs, Education, Evidence, and Raw Feeding

FEEDING EGGS TO DOGS

When I first started feeding a raw diet, people were shocked to learn I was adding eggs to my dogs' meals. Eggs will cause a biotin deficiency, eggs have salmonella, and eggs will increase my dog's cholesterol levels.

Maybe. Nope. NOPE!!!!

I feed eggs (chicken, duck, and quail) to add additional protein and healthy fat to the bowl, along with…

- Vitamin A – eyesight, bone growth, and immune system
- Vitamin B2 – helps to convert food into fuel
- Vitamin B9 – formation of red blood cells, protein metabolism
- Vitamin B12 – nerve functions
- Iron – blood production and energy
- Selenium – behaves as an antioxidant in the body
- Fatty Acids – brain functions, skin and coat health, joints, and immune system

I prefer pasture-raised eggs because they're more nutritious and higher in beneficial fatty acids.

Egg Whites Only: it's not a good idea to feed raw egg whites only because the avidin in egg whites is a protein that binds biotin, leading to a biotin deficiency.

I have yet to hear of a dog developing a biotin deficiency, but this doesn't mean it can't happen. In the raw feeding community, there are pet parents who admit to having some concern over the risk based on how their dog absorbs nutrients.

I now cook eggs for my dogs. Several people recommended lightly cooking the eggs (poached or soft-boiled) because it'll cook the whites enough to stop the avidin from binding with the biotin while leaving the yolks liquid.

Feeding Raw Eggs to Dogs: you can still feed raw eggs to your dogs; I still do on occasion. I crack it over their meal or mix a raw egg in their kefir on milk-fast days.

Feeding Raw Egg Shells: I don't feed the eggshells to my dogs because none of them will eat them. Some raw feeders add dried eggshells as a source of calcium; I don't believe eggshells are an adequate substitution for bones. So, I dry them out and add them to my flower and vegetable garden for nutrients and to ward off slugs.

How Often I Feed Eggs: I typically add a raw egg to my dogs' meals three to four days a week. This is my preference, not a rule. I lightly cook eggs for two of my dogs. My senior dogs prefer scrambled eggs fed separately from his meal.

- Pasture-raised chicken eggs are fed three to four days a week.
- Pasture-raised duck eggs are rich and can lead to gas, so I only feed them once a week.
- I feed quail eggs three times a week, feeding two at a time, or one in each meal (I feed twice daily).
- Quail eggs aren't a regular in my dogs' diet.

Where I Source Eggs: I live in a rural area with plenty of farms and homesteaders. I'm able to source pasture-raised chicken and duck eggs from friends. I get quail eggs from a local Asian market.

If you're looking for a source, check Craigslist or the Facebook Marketplace. Check the reviews before placing an order.

EDUCATING OURSELVES ABOUT RAW FEEDING

Many of us are learning how to feed our dogs a raw diet via the Internet, and it's not easy. There is a lot of conflicting information, and everyone thinks they're experts. While it may be tempting to leave a comment for your favorite blogger, vlogger, or veterinarian, I have a better suggestion.

JOIN A RAW FEEDING GROUP

You may have to test a few out before you find one (or two) that are a good fit for you, but this is your best way to get answers to your questions.

If you're having trouble finding sources, you can find other raw feeders who live in or near your town in a raw feeding group.

If you have questions about "balance," no problem, many raw feeding groups are managed by pet parents who offer meal formulation services.

If you have several "stupid" questions, you can search the discussions in a raw feeding group and quickly see many people had the same question.

There are many raw feeding groups on Facebook. I highly recommend Raw Feeding 101 – Learn to Feed Raw.

After a decade of feeding raw, I find it's too overwhelming when I'm a member of too many groups.

FOLLOW RAW FEEDERS ON INSTAGRAM

I love following raw feeders on Instagram because I learn a lot from their shared meals. Many share recipes, sourcing tips, and more. It's important to remember the meals are beautiful for social media – so we can see what's in the bowl. We don't have to do the same for our dogs at home.

CHECK OUT MY RESOURCES LIST

I maintain a list of the people I follow, my favorite books, and more on my blog. To check it out, visit
KeepTheTailWagging.com/Resources

EVIDENCE RAW FEEDING IS BENEFICIAL FOR DOGS

For many, the mountains of anecdotal evidence proving the benefits of raw feeding aren't enough. And while there are a growing number of organizations studying the benefits of raw feeding, there currently isn't a widely respected, long-term study.

In other words, nothing has been published that would be excepted by the majority of the traditional veterinarian community or the big pet food outfits.

I did sign my dogs up or the ongoing Long Living Pets Research Project that is managed by Thomas Sandberg. Besides this project, you can also find science-based information in the book, Feeding Dogs, Dr. Conor Brady.

LACK OF FUNDING = LACK OF STUDIES

While there are limited studies on raw feeding, critics of raw feeding believe that leaders in the community are cherry picking facts to meet their desire to prove that raw feeding is superior to dry dog food.

I was convinced when Rodrigo's health issues gradually went away and stayed away. I didn't need a scientific study to explain why my dog lived ten years longer than his first veterinarian predicted.

F - Fear, Fermentation, Fish and Fish Oil,
Fasting, and Raw Feeding

FEAR OF FEEDING RAW TO DOGS

Many people new to raw feeding are scared out of their minds and I was one of them. It didn't matter how many people told me my dogs would be fine and raw feeding was easy; I didn't believe them. Not one of them.

I was afraid to feed my dogs raw because…

I thought raw feeding would be complicated.

I thought raw feeding would be expensive.

I thought my vet would shame me for trying to kill my dogs.

I thought my dogs would choke on a bone or break a tooth.

I stumbled for the first year as I learned about raw feeding. Connecting with other raw feeders and learning I wasn't alone helped me overcome my fears. Thanks to social media, I have a lot of great friends who feed raw. It's cool to be able to compare notes and ask random questions without the fear of being judged or made to feel stupid.

If you're afraid to take the plunge and transition your dog to a raw food diet, I suggest connecting with local raw feeders. Sometimes, talking with someone one-on-one and seeing how they feed their dogs helps you see raw feeding isn't so scary.

FERMENTED FOODS FOR DOGS

I add fermented foods to my dogs' diet regularly to support our dogs' gut health and immune system. Plus, fermented foods help the system to naturally detox.

Fermented foods are generally found in the refrigerated section of natural grocery stores — look for brands that don't have onions.

There are many DIY recipes for fermented foods with shredded vegetables, and they don't require much salt. You can also choose to use a culture starter in place of salt.

THE FERMENTED FOODS I FEED TO MY DOGS

- Raw goat's milk
- Kefir
- Fermented fish broth
- Homemade yogurt

I don't make fermented vegetables often, but it is an easy process and you can find a recipe on KeepTheTailWagging.com.

FEEDING FISH TO DOGS

Some may be nervous about feeding raw fish too dogs. If you're not, look for YouTube videos showing worms in fish. #yuck

I don't have an issue feeding fish (raw or cooked) to my dogs, but I have a few "rules" to make fish safe.

1 - I cook salmon or steelhead trout from the Pacific Ocean before feeding it to my dogs because the fish may contain flukes infected with bacterium that may lead to "salmon poisoning" in dogs.

2 – I don't add fish to my DIY blends when doing meal prep. Storing fish (combining it in a raw blend) that contain thiaminase deactivates the thiamin (Vitamin B1) in meat, leading to a deficiency over time.

Fish that Don't Contain Thiaminase

- Flounder
- Haddock
- Halibut, Atlantic
- Herring, Lake

- Mackerel, Atlantic
- Oysters
- Pollock
- Rainbow Trout
- Salmon, Atlantic
- Salmon, Coho
- Shrimp
- Smelt, Pond
- Squid
- Yellowtail

FISH OIL FOR RAW FED DOGS

Fish oil is great for skin/coat health, joint health (reverses inflammation), brain and neurological health, and heart health.

Dogs can't produce their own Omega 3 fatty acids, so they need to get it from their diet. There are three common types:

- ALA (α-linolenic acid): these are found in plants like hemp, camelina, and flaxseed.
- EPA (eicosatetraenoic acid) and DHA (docosahexaenoic acid): EPA and DHA partner together and come from sources like fish, eggs, and krill (the teeny fish that follow whales around).

When adding Omega-3 fatty acids to the bowl, I prefer fish or salmon oil to a plant-based oil. The ALA in plants must be converted to EPA/DHA in a dog's system. I prefer to avoid this extra step and go directly for EPA/ DHA.

Today, I feed fish to my dogs, but more as a protein source. I feed a Wild Alaska salmon oil product that comes in the right bottle minimizes oxidation. By doing this, I know my dogs are getting a quality source of Omega-3 fatty acids that meets their nutritional needs as well as Vitamin D and E.

Other sources of Omega 3 fatty acids include pasture-raised chicken and duck eggs, sardines, mackerel, squid, green lipped mussels, and salmon.

While oysters also contain Omega 3 fatty acids, it's not enough for my dogs, but I do feed oysters as an additional source of zinc.

G - Gut Health, Green Tripe, Guidelines and Raw Feeding

GUT HEALTH AND RAW FEEDING

Fresh food is more bioavailable and easier to digest. The living enzymes support a healthier gut microbiome while alleviating the stress on the pancreas. Vegetables are a great source of fiber and serve as food for the gut microbiome.

I don't recommend starting a raw food diet with digestive supplements unless advised by a veterinarian experienced in canine nutrition. So much in a fresh food diet supports gut health and digestive supplements may not be necessary. After having my dog's microbiome tested, I learned the probiotics and bacteria in digestive supplements could replace the native bacteria in a dog's gut – something we don't want to happen. So, I only use digestive supplements when one of my dogs needs additional support – not as a daily addition to the bowl.

Because more of the nutrients are absorbed in a fresh food diet than in a kibble diet, the poop is smaller and less smelly. Don't get me wrong, the poop still smells, just not as bad as kibble poop.

A few more foods, other than your typical raw meal, which support gut health include:

- Raw goat's milk
- Kefir
- Fermented foods
- Homemade plain yogurt
- Vegetables
- Chia seeds

Remember this mantra: "Healthy Gut, Healthy Dog"

GREEN TRIPE AND RAW FEEDING

Green tripe is the stomach of ruminating animals like cows, bison, deer, and sheep.

Benefits of Green Tripe: I give our dogs green tripe because it's a smelly treat they love. I used to believe green tripe could be a temporary substitution for bone (WRONG) and I fed green tripe because I believed my dogs would benefit from the digestive enzymes (QUESTIONABLE).

Today, I feed green tripe as a muscle meat, feeding it as a side, a meal topper, or a light lunch.

Not All Dogs Can Eat Green Tripe: Some dogs can only handle green tripe in small doses; feeding too much will lead to diarrhea. They may not have a sensitivity; green tripe is simply too rich for them. By adding a pound or two of green tripe to my meal prep, my sensitive dogs can tolerate it better and enjoy the benefits.

Where to Source Green Tripe: I order green tripe through a local raw food co-op. Several brands offer frozen and freeze-dried green tripe. To find a co-op in your area, you can look for your state on KeepTheTailWagging.com/coop.

Canned Green Tripe: I no longer give our dogs canned green tripe because (1) it's cooked, so I question the existence of the enzymes, (2) some brands add carrageenan gum, which has been tied to health issues in pets, and (3) it's more expensive than buying actual green tripe.

GUIDELINES OF RAW FEEDING

I made many mistakes when I started feeding raw. The biggest one was failing to adjust the diet to my dogs' individual needs.

A few other guidelines I've found helpful are:

- Be open to new information.
- Understand there isn't one diet for all dogs.
- It's okay if your dog doesn't want to eat raw; try lightly cooking.

Only you are the expert on your dog.

FEED THE DOG IN FRONT OF YOU

As I became more confident in feeding raw, I adjusted their diets to meet their various needs at a moment's notice. It's not as complicated as it was when I first started feeding a raw diet. Raw feeding became easier when I stopped overthinking every step and trusted myself to feed my dogs.

H - Holistic Veterinarians and Raw Feeding

A FEW THINGS I'VE LEARNED ABOUT HOLISTIC VETERINARIANS

A holistic or integrative veterinarian can be an amazing resource for raw feeding. Our veterinarian and her team have been supportive of the choices I've made for our dogs and helpful over the years.

Holistic veterinarians are more expensive than traditional veterinarians; sometimes. I only take the dogs to the vet once a year, with Rodrigo going twice yearly for a wellness exam and blood work. Because I'm not going to the vet all the time, I am saving more than spending.

Holistic and integrative veterinarian medicine is covered by the best pet insurance companies. Our pet insurance company covers alternative medicine like acupuncture, homeopathy, massage therapy, and more.

Pet insurance won't cover titer tests or blood work.

Not all holistic vets are down with raw feeding. They may not be pushing prescription pet food down your throat, but they won't jump up and down because you've chosen to feed your dog raw meat.

I believe holistic medicine is a great partner to traditional medicine. For example, Scout has gone through chemotherapy (traditional), and he also gets acupuncture and Chinese herbs (holistic). These modalities are working together to improve his outcome.

3 WAYS TO FIND A HOLISTIC VETERINARIAN

SEARCH ONLINE

With online reviews, it's a lot easier to find a holistic vet. If you discover a vet with low stars (3 instead of 5), check for reviews left by unhappy former clients. Yelp allows businesses to respond to reviews — it's good reading.

SEARCH THE AHVMA

The American Holistic Veterinary Medical Association (AHVMA) has a directory of holistic veterinarians. Remember the list isn't exhaustive; not all holistic vets are listed.

ASK FOR A REFERRAL

If you have connected with raw feeders in your area, ask them for a referral to a holistic veterinarian. What I like about this method is I can ask someone about their experience instead of figuring out if an online review is genuine.

I - Introducing a Raw Fed Dog to a New Veterinarian

CONFESSING YOU'RE A RAW FEEDER

I recognize my fortune when it comes to veterinarians. Not everyone can speak to their veterinarians about raw feeding. Maybe this can help.

I've been able to change the mind of every veterinarian who saw our dogs who was initially against raw feeding by doing one thing – asking them to share their concerns and then addressing each one.

Bacteria: If they're worried about bacteria, I assure them I clean everything, and I remind them of the other places where dogs can be exposed to salmonella, including kibble.

Nutritionally Complete: If they are worried about balance, I explain how I balance my dogs' diet – by using Animal Diet Formulator software and maintaining a nutrient spreadsheet to become familiar with the food I feed. I follow up by having my dogs nutrient-tested to ensure I'm on the right track.

Sourcing: If they're worried about my sourcing, I share that I get the meat from local farms.

Education: If they're worried I'll stop learning about dog nutrition, I share the books I'm following – leaning heavily on the ones authored or coauthored by a veterinarian.

Ultimately, the proof was my dogs. I've had veterinarians change their minds about raw feeding after examining my dogs.

Meeting a new vet doesn't have to be a negative experience. With each interaction, I learned something new. And if a veterinarian wasn't a good fit, I moved on to the next.

J - Joint Health, Canine Arthritis, and Raw Feeding

ARTHRITIS SUCKS

Rodrigo developed arthritic symptoms when he was two years old and fed kibble. The limping and other signs of joint pain went away shortly after we switched to raw.

This is what I've learned about supporting my dogs' joints naturally:

- While duck feet, trachea, tendons, and bone broth are healthy for dogs, I don't think they can replace a quality joint supplement for a dog with arthritis.

- Adding foods like duck feet, trachea, bone broth, etc., which support joint health to the diet is better than adding nothing; plus, I believe these foods do go far to keep healthy joints healthy and slow down degeneration.

- I believe in adding a joint supplement to my dogs' diet before they show signs of needing a joint supplement. I start giving my dogs joint supplements at the age of three.

- CBD oil is great for pain management in some dogs, but it doesn't support joint health alone. It may take some time to find the right CBD oil product for your dog and I recommend alternating between two or three brands. The brands I use are listed on KeepTheTailWagging.com.

FOODS THAT SUPPORT JOINT HEALTH

I'm a big fan of fish and feed it to my dogs several days a week. Sardines, salmon, trout, and mackerel are favorites. I also give my dogs green-lipped mussel treats.

Duck feet, rabbit feet, beef backstrap, and beef tendons also support joint health.

And I make a lot of bone broth, which I feed several days a week, especially during the winter (comfort food).

K - Knowledge, Kicked Out, Kibble, and Raw Feeding

SHARING YOUR KNOWLEDGE ABOUT RAW FEEDING

When it comes to raw feeding, unless you feed a 100% premade raw diet or have someone who can work with you, homework will be required. I read books, I grilled many veterinarians with questions, I followed leaders in the raw feeding community, and I joined Facebook groups. All of these resources helped me grow from a person who was worried she'd harm her dogs to someone who makes raw food while binge-watching television.

I don't have a "my way or the highway" mentality regarding raising dogs. If a Facebook friend shares a picture of a bag of kibble, I don't send a private message or leave a comment critiquing their choices in dog food and recommending raw. From personal experience, it's better to ask people if they're interested in my thoughts than push my thoughts on them.

Don't assume people feed kibble out of ignorance. There are many reasons why someone won't home cook or feed raw to their dogs.

Don't hate on people for not feeding raw. I see this daily in Facebook groups, people judging friends, family members, and strangers for feeding kibble. I admit I have judged people as well, but then I take a step back and remind myself when I brought Rodrigo and Sydney home, I was proud of my research on kibble brands.

Be open to other perspectives. We're constantly learning new things about canine nutrition, and if someone has success with a certain diet, if I hear of long-living dogs, I want to know more and may adopt the new information if it's a good fit for my dogs. You'll be amazed at what you'll learn that will improve your dog's diet.

Continue sharing content about the benefits of raw feeding. While it may seem like no one is listening, one day, a friend will have a question about dog nutrition, and you'll be their resource because you're always sharing articles and blog posts on the topic.

BEING KICKED OUT OF A RAW FEEDING GROUP

If you're an inquisitive person like me, then you will be kicked out of a raw feeding group eventually.

To make navigating the world of Facebook raw feeding groups easier, I offer the following suggestions:

- Follow their rules. It doesn't matter if they don't make sense; it's their group.
- Search the group before posting; sometimes, the same question is asked repeatedly.
- Don't argue with members about their ideas; instead, ask them what led them to make their choices. It's amazing what you can learn.

Facebook raw feeding groups are a fantastic place to learn more about raw feeding, connect with other raw feeders, and chat with people who understand why you feed raw. Not every group is for every raw feeder; take your time, and you'll find the right group for you and your dogs.

FEEDING KIBBLE AND FRESH FOOD

In 2020, while everyone was clearing grocery store shelves of toilet paper, I was standing in a local independent pet food store with a confused expression on my face. I was there to buy a few bags of kibble because people were worried that supply chain slowdowns would make it harder to buy meat for our dogs.

Feeding kibble isn't the end of the world. But, with my dogs' health history, I prefer to feed them fresh food. However, if I find myself in a position where raw feeding is no longer feasible, I will do the following to improve the quality of the kibble I feed to my dogs:

I'll choose baked or air-dried dog food instead of traditional kibble.

I'll feed fresh food to my dogs: ground beef/turkey/etc., bone broth, kefir, raw goat's milk, canned sardines, canned oysters, low glycemic vegetables, berries, apples, and poached eggs.

L - Liver, Liver Health, and Raw Feeding

FEEDING LIVER TO MY DOGS

Liver is a favorite treat in our house, and grass-fed beef liver is a staple in my dogs' diet.

The liver contains nutrients like folate, iron, vitamin A, vitamin B, and copper.

LIVER AND LIVER HEALTH

Feeding liver also supports liver health. However, if your dog has copper storage hepatopathy or abnormal accumulation of copper, feeding liver can be tricky. I've been told by veterinarians that feeding too much liver can negatively affect the liver of healthy dogs. Speak to your holistic vet about supporting your dog's liver health through diet.

LIVER AND DIARRHEA

The liver is a rich meat, and feeding too much can result in diarrhea or loose stool. When adding it to a puppy's diet and the raw diet of a dog new to raw feeding, it's important to start small and build up. I've learned to start puppies and small dogs at 1/3 tsp and start larger dogs at 1/2 tsp, working up to 5% of their diet.

LIVER AND DETOX

A liver's job is to clear all the toxins from an animal's system. Some people have warned me some liver can make my dogs sick due to the toxins. I won't accept liver from wild animals (my friends who hunt); to be safe, I stick with human-grade liver.

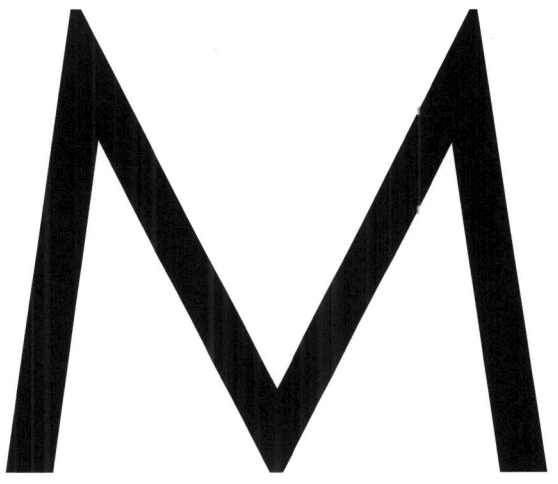

M - Models of Raw Feeding for Dogs

MODELS OF RAW FEEDING

When you join the raw feeding community, it doesn't take long to realize no one feeds raw the same way. Over the years, I've fed premade raw, BARF Model, FrankenPrey Model, FrankenBARF, and Rotational MonoFeeding.

Today, I've created a routine that works great for my dogs and takes something from many raw feeding models.

The pros and cons of each diet I list below are based on my experience. Not all raw feeders will agree. And some of this may be outdated – not all raw feeders are married to these models.

PREMADE RAW DOG FOOD

So premade raw isn't considered a "model" of raw feeding, but with the growth of the raw sector over the years, I think it deserves mention. Premade Raw Dog Food is commercial raw you buy at a local, independent pet store, order online, or buy directly from brands.

BENEFITS OF FEEDING PREMADE RAW

-   We don't have to worry about balancing the diet.
-   Access to more proteins.
-   No need to buy extra freezers to store bulk orders unless you have a lot of big dogs.
-   It's quick and easy to feed with little mess; plus, it can be fed in a dog dish.
-   Some brands deliver to your door.

DOWNSIDES OF FEEDING PREMADE RAW

-   Some premade raw brands use HPP (high-pressure pasteurization) processing to kill off bacteria. At the same

time, this makes raw feeding an option for more people —
my opinion is the processing may kill off living enzymes too.
It's been around for a while and the process has improved.

- Feeding premade raw is expensive because the brand takes
  care of sourcing and balancing for you.
- Some premade raw brands use synthetic vitamins to make the
  diet balanced. Depending on the amount used and the
  sourcing, this can be a negative.
- Some premade raw brands source from factory farms. This is
  a deal breaker for some raw feeders.
- In the first iteration of this book, I identified the fact that a
  commercial raw brand would balance to AAFCO standards
  as a negative. Today, I have a better understanding of the pet
  food industry. Two reasons why it's great some brands
  choose to balance their diets to AFFCO standards. This step
  will…
- Satisfy pet parents that are looking for some evidence that
  the food will meet their dogs' nutritional needs.
- Satisfy veterinarians who believe a raw food diet doesn't
  meet a dog's nutritional needs.

BARF MODEL RAW FEEDING

BARF (biologically appropriate raw food) model raw feeding
includes: 65%-75% muscle meat, 10%-15% bone, 5% liver, 5%
offal (secreting organs like kidney and spleen), 5%-10% fruits,
vegetables, dairy

If you search ratios for the BARF model, you'll find several ranges,
with muscle meat as low as 45% and bone content as high as 50%.
The BARF model also encourages supplementation when needed.

BENEFITS OF FEEDING BARF MODEL

- Dogs have more access to antioxidants, fiber, and other
  nutrients by adding vegetables, fruit, dairy, and supplements.

- Easier to meet your dog's nutritional needs because vegetation and supplements are acceptable.
- Ground raw dog food is acceptable and easier (and cleaner) to feed.
- Raw meaty bones and recreational bones are added separately for teeth cleaning.

DOWNSIDES TO FEEDING BARF MODEL

- Dogs eat faster because ground raw is easier to gulp.
- Ground raw doesn't offer the teeth cleaning benefits of eating whole raw.
- Must have storage to buy in bulk, which makes raw feeding more affordable.
- To make nutrients in vegetables more bioavailable, there is the extra step of breaking the cellular wall (freeze, puree, or blanched).
- Some dogs won't eat vegetables.
- You might need to invest in a meat grinder if you feed DIY.

PREY MODEL RAW FEEDING

Prey model raw feeding follows the 80/10/10 rule of feeding raw; 80% muscle meat, 10% bone, 5% liver, and 5% offal (secreting organs like kidney and spleen).

When I was new to raw feeding, the Prey model discourages using vegetables, fruit, dairy, and over supplementation. Dogs can get everything they need through diet. For example, instead of fish oil, feed sardines and mackerel. Instead of a digestive supplement, trust the living enzymes in raw food and add green tripe.

BENEFITS OF FEEDING PREY MODEL

- Dogs are eating in a way that is more reminiscent of wolves.

- Whole raw allows dogs to satisfy their chew drive, clean their teeth, and work their jaw and shoulder muscles.
- Dogs take longer to finish their meal, which is great for their digestive system.
- It's less expensive without the supplements.

DOWNSIDES TO FEEDING PREY MODEL

- Must have storage to buy in bulk, which makes raw feeding more affordable.
- Ground raw dog food isn't always acceptable in this model.
- Feeding whole raw can be challenging for some people/dogs.

FRANKENBARF MODEL RAW FEEDING

The FrankenBARF model might follow 80/10/10 with 80% muscle meat, 10% bone, 5% liver, 5% offal (secreting organs like kidney and spleen). I always thought FrankenBARF (or FrankenPrey) meant I modified the BARF diet to meet the needs of my dogs. Nope. As you can guess "Franken" means parts from various animals that are combined to make a meal.

Fruits, vegetables, kefir, raw eggs, and supplements are added to the above to provide additional nutrients and satisfy each dog's specific needs.

BENEFITS OF FEEDING FRANKENBARF MODEL

- It's easier to meet the needs of each of my dogs when I modify the BARF model.
- Dogs have more access to nutrients by adding vegetables, fruit, dairy, and supplements.
- Easier to meet my dogs' nutritional needs.
- Ground raw dog food is acceptable and easier to feed. However, whole raw is fed, satisfying a dog's chew drive and cleaning their teeth.

- Raw meaty bones and recreational bones are added separately for teeth cleaning.

DOWNSIDES TO FEEDING FRANKENBARF MODEL

- A lot of time goes into grinding meat (with the wrong grinder) and mixing ingredients; a quality meat grinder is a must if you plan to feed ground raw.
- Must have storage to buy in bulk, which makes raw feeding more affordable.
- To make nutrients in vegetables more bioavailable, it's better to freeze, puree, or blanch (boiled for a few minutes) vegetables – which can be more work.

ROTATIONAL MONOFEEDING (RMF)

Rotational MonoFeeding (RMF) is a diet I was introduced to in 2021, and I considered switching my dogs to this model because I agree with several tenants.

RMF is a model created by Nora Lenz and follows the belief that since dogs have one chamber in their stomach to digest food, they should be fed meat separately from vegetables.

Nora Lenz took inspiration from wild dogs and wolves and, through RMF, encourages pet parents to feed meat on one day (the kill), vegetables (foraging), and fasting (when food is unavailable). The Rotational MonoFeeding book offers several feeding regimens based on pet parents' goals for their dogs.

BENEFITS OF ROTATIONAL MONOFEEDING

- Easier on the digestive system.
- Incorporates fasting in the diet.
- Meal prep is easier.
- There isn't stress to "balance" the diet.

- A meat order lasts longer.

DOWNSIDES TO ROTATIONAL MONOFEEDING

- The diet may not meet all of your dog's nutritional needs; balancing the diet can be challenging.
- Supplements are discouraged.
- Bone broth and fat (coconut oil, fish oil, raw goat's milk, kefir) are discouraged.
- Feeding full meals of sweet potatoes or fruit is questionable – is this species appropriate? I don't think so.

I'm new to RMF, and while I find some of the beliefs put forward by Nora Lenz to be compelling and, in some cases, spot on, I don't believe a full adaptation of RMF is appropriate for my dogs.

Instead, I decided to add vegetables as an option on the "modified fasting" day - my dogs ate their vegetable meal once. They turned away from subsequent vegetable-only meals. They like vegetables, but not as the main part of their diet.

CHOOSING THE RIGHT MODEL FOR YOUR DOG

All raw feeding models will have a community that follows all or most of its tenants with varying degrees of success.

I learned as much as I could about each model, tried them with my dogs, and finally settled on a modified model that incorporated everything I learned. This model is the best fit for my dogs, my budget, and our geographical location (for sourcing).

I remain flexible and open to new ideas because as my dogs age, their nutritional needs change. And, if we add a new dog to our family, they may need something different.

N - Natural Vitamins, New Proteins, and Raw Feeding

NATURAL VITAMINS AND RAW FEEDING

I do not believe in adding a multivitamin to my dogs' diet. My dogs can get the bulk of their nutrients from whole food. But it's still important to know where our dogs are getting their nutrients from.

The below table offers sources of various vitamins and minerals. This is not an exhaustive list; it's simply here to show you what you're adding to the bowl.

Vitamin A: skin, vision, immune system — raw eggs, liver, spinach, kale, broccoli, carrots, greens, pumpkin

Vitamin B: overall growth of our dogs — spirulina, raw goat milk, kefir

Vitamin C: immune system — kale, broccoli

Vitamin D: regulates calcium and phosphorous levels — fatty fish, raw goat milk, liver, beef

Vitamin E: cell function, fat metabolism, anti-oxidant — liver, kale, spinach, greens, broccoli, parsley

Vitamin K: healthy blood functions — kale, cabbage, broccoli, kefir, asparagus

Calcium: Phosphorous: strong teeth and bones, supports heart, muscle, and never functions — green tripe, egg shells

Iron: blood health, energy, immune system — red meat, liver, eggs

Magnesium: healthy bones, muscles, nerve systems, enzyme functions —broccoli, green beans

Although I balance my adult dogs' diet over time, I still work to meet their nutritional needs, and if I had to keep track of all the nutrients in every drop of food I added to the bowl, I'd be tempted to run screaming from the house.

I prefer EASY when it comes to raw feeding. So, to make sure I'm meeting my dogs' nutritional needs...

- Use a base mix without grains or potatoes – Dr. Harvey's
- I use meal formulator software – Animal Diet Formulator
- I confirmed my dogs' diet is nutritionally complete through hair/mineral testing - ParsleyPet - and working with a certified canine nutritionist.

THE PROBLEM WITH SYNTHETIC VITAMINS

When I see a brand is using synthetic vitamins, I don't run away screaming in horror. Synthetic vitamins in small amount don't concern me. However, if the bulk the ingredients were created in a laboratory, then the food isn't for my dogs.

Synthetic vitamins are less bioavailable and, because they're isolated, they aren't as beneficial.

The best example I've been given is Vitamin C. When we (the humans) get our Vitamin C from an orange, we also get the other nutrients in the orange that make the Vitamin C so effective. Yeah, I might have to eat more oranges, but in the long run, I believe this is better for my overall health.

NEW PROTEINS AND RAW FEEDING

I like to alternate between at least five proteins when feeding my dogs. This is a personal preference and not a requirement for raw feeding.

- Duck
- Pork
- Beef
- Quail
- Rabbit

- Fish

I chose proteins based on what my dogs can eat and what I can afford.

Before trying a new protein, I learn as much as possible to determine where it'll fit within their diet, including nutrient profile, benefits, sourcing, and energy (warming/cooling).

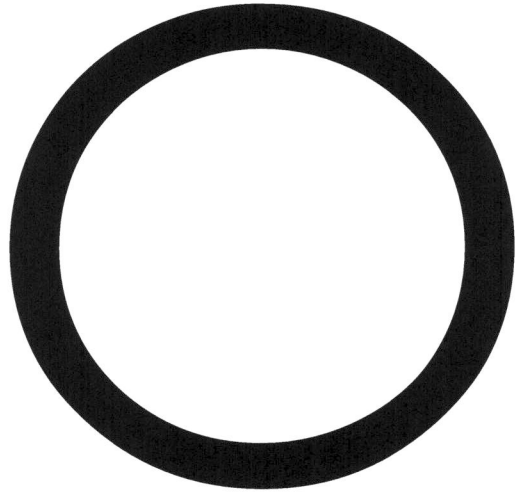

O - Organ Meat, Offal, and Raw Feeding

ORGAN MEAT VS. OFFAL IN RAW FEEDING

There are several charts online listing which organs are fed as meat (organ meat) and which are fed as secreting organs (offal). However, I call it all organ meat. I seek a variety of both in my dogs' diet and often feed:

- beef heart (organ meat)
- beef tongue (organ meat)
- beef lungs (organ meat)
- beef liver (offal)
- beef spleen (offal)
- beef pancreas (offal)
- green tripe (organ meat)
- pork heart (organ meat)
- duck gizzards (organ meat)
- bison testicles (offal)

WHY WE FEED ORGAN MEAT TO DOGS

Organ meat is packed with nutrients and the least expensive part of my dogs' diet, so they never go without.

- Vitamins: A, B, D, E, and K
- Minerals: calcium, phosphorus, magnesium, manganese, iron, copper, iodine, potassium, sodium, selenium, and zinc
- Omega-3 fats EPA and DHA

QUALITY SOURCES FOR ORGAN MEAT

The best sources for offal include local raw food co-ops, farms, homesteaders, butchers, and Ethnic markets.

HOW I FEED ORGAN MEAT TO MY DOGS

I incorporate organs in my meal prep, adding two pounds of a beef organ blend with every 6-8 pounds of ground beef and bone.

I also give our dogs freeze-dried organ treats. Not enough to meet a nutritional need, but enough to make them happy.

HOW MUCH ORGAN MEAT I FEED TO MY DOGS

How much organ meat I feed varies on what I have available and how much food I'm making for my dogs. When I'm low on organ meat, I use more base mix. I don't add more organ meat to the next meal prep to avoid diarrhea.

I don't mind feeding more than 10% organ meat to my dogs and feel comfortable feeding as much as 15% at times. I don't measure this out; when feeding 80/10/10, I guesstimate.

WHAT IF MY DOG WON'T EAT ORGAN MEAT

Some dogs don't like the texture of organ meat; for these dogs, you can try the following:

- Try grinding the organ meat and mixing it into a raw blend.
- Lightly cook organ meat.

P - Pork, Parasites, Pancreas, and Raw Feeding

FEEDING PORK IN A RAW FOOD DIET

Human-grade pork is perfectly safe to feed. Trichinosis hasn't been found in the human feed chain in decades. I wouldn't feed wild pork to my dogs. I primarily feed pork as a main ingredient. However, sometimes, I mix it with a lean protein (rabbit, venison, elk, bison, beef) to keep the amount of fat in the meal reasonable.

PARASITES AND RAW FEEDING

Dogs are equipped to handle bacteria due to an enzyme in their saliva that kills bacteria, a highly acidic gut makes it difficult for bacteria to thrive, and a shorter digestive tract equipped to absorb nutrients and push food through quickly.

BUT WHAT ABOUT PARASITES?

The only food in my freezers with a risk of parasites are wild game and raw fish. I rarely feed wild game, but fish is a regular part of my dogs' diet. Either way, I freeze the meat for at least three weeks to kill any parasites.

I live in a rural area, and my dogs have killed wild animals. When this happens, I monitor their stool for any tale-tale signs of parasites.

There are whole foods you can add to your dog's diet that will help rid the body of parasites, like:

- Pumpkin seeds (go easy because these can cause cramps)
- Garlic (see Letter V to learn more)
- Apple cider vinegar
- Bone broth

Some people recommend diatomaceous earth (DE), a white powder derived from the fossilized remains of marine phytoplankton. When it comes into contact with parasites, it dehydrates their bodies, killing them, so they pass through a dog's digestive system in the stool.

However, once DE is introduced to a damp environment (our digestive system), it may no longer effective. My concern is how drying DE can be, so I no longer use it on or around my dogs.

I can't confirm these natural remedies are effective because I haven't seen evidence of this with my dogs.

PANCREAS AND RAW FEEDING

Rodrigo was diagnosed with exocrine pancreatic insufficiency (EPI) in 2019. His pancreas isn't producing digestive enzymes, making it impossible for him to absorb nutrients no matter how much he eats. If left untreated, he would starve to death.

SYMPTOMS OF EPI INCLUDE

- Continued weight loss despite always being hungry
- Pooping more often than the other dogs; poop is larger, yellow or gray in color, and soft
- Dog eats poop (coprophagy)
- Increased gas and tummy noises
- Occasional diarrhea and vomiting
- Increased anxiety, fearful behavior

A veterinarian can conduct a test to confirm EPI by testing a stool sample for the presence of digestive enzymes.

I add digestive enzymes to all of Rodrigo's meals. I mix it in and allow it to sit and predigest over 15 minutes and then feed.

PANCREAS SUPPLEMENT vs. RAW PANCREAS

I want to try adding raw pancreas to my dog's diet. However, it's a bit high maintenance and challenging for me to source.

I've been advised to add 2 ounces of pancreas for every 20 pounds of body weight. I was warned, feeding more not recommended and can cause damage to the pancreas.

To maximize enzyme efficiency, we need to whip the pancreas with a fork or wire whisk to a pudding-like consistency or liquefy in a blender.

Pancreas needs to be served at room temperature.

Pancreas has a shelf life of only three months which I'll have to consider when ordering.

I only feed raw pancreas as part of an organ blend. It's not enough to allow me to skip the enzyme supplement.

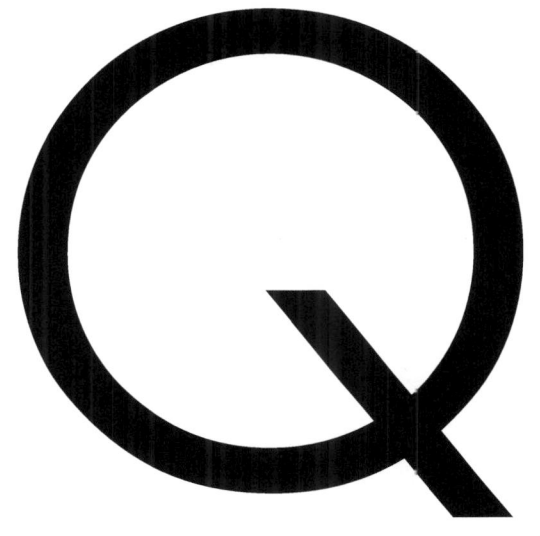

Q - Quality Brands, Questions, and Raw Feeding

FINDING QUALITY RAW DOG FOOD BRANDS

If you're looking for quality raw food brands, your best resource is your local, independent pet store. The store owner or manager can direct you to the best brands. I've learned independent store owners research every product they add to their store.

Your second-best resource is other raw feeders. But if you ask for recommendations in a raw feeding group, be prepared to get overwhelmed because there are a lot of great brands out there.

QUESTIONS ABOUT RAW FEEDING

Although the raw feeding learning curve isn't as steep as it was several years ago, I still have a lot to learn, and I will always have questions. The following helps:

- It's good to have a vet experienced with (or open to) raw feeding.
- Join a friendly raw feeding group open to answering questions and exploring all aspects of raw feeding.
- Look for opportunities to learn more — books, webinars, seminars, and workshops.
- And network with other local raw feeders to share experiences and tips.

We never stop learning.

R - Recreational Bones, Raw Meaty Bones, and Raw Feeding

FEEDING MY DOGS RAW BONES

When I began feeding my dogs a raw diet, I knew raw bones were part of the menu, but I was nervous because…

- raw bones can break teeth
- raw bones can splinter and cause injury
- raw bones can become impacted

It took me a while to become comfortable with feeding raw bones to my dogs. One day, I decided to allow my control-freak flag to fly, and I allowed my dogs to try various bones, a new one each weekend.

This taught me the bones that weren't a good fit for them and the safe ones.

FINDING SAFE RAW BONES FOR DOGS

I always supervise my dogs when they're eating their raw bones. I always keep a high-value treat on hand if I need to step in and swap a bone out because it's not a good fit.

After a few weeks of testing out bones, I found raw bones that were a good fit for my dogs:

- lamb necks
- duck necks (eaten with meals)
- duck feet (eaten with meals)
- duck frames
- rabbit legs
- pork ribs
- whole quail (more meat than bone)

BENEFITS OF FEEDING RAW BONES TO DOGS

While there are several health benefits to feeding raw bones to dogs, I'll admit I give them to my dogs to get a block of quiet in a house with four dogs.

A raw bone keeps the dogs still, quiet, and focused on their chewing. I can work on my blog, read a book, or enjoy a nice afternoon.

Since this isn't all about me, let me share other reasons raw bones are good for my dogs.

- Cleans their teeth and gums.
- Strengthens their neck and shoulder muscles.
- Satisfies their chew drive.
- And, in the case of raw meaty bones, provides a small meal, making it a great option on a modified fasting day.

ALTERNATIVES TO RAW BONES FOR DOGS

I feed my dogs the messier raw bones outside. In the winter, it's too cold to supervise their bone chewing outside, and my better half isn't comfortable with me laying tarps around the house for inside enjoyment. So, I give my dogs air-dried chews from Real Dog Box.

The alternatives we give to our dogs keep the plaque down and occupy our dogs while satisfying their chew drive, but not always as well as raw bones.

S - Supplements and Raw Feeding

WHY I ADD SUPPLEMENTS TO MY DOGS' DIET

My dogs get the bulk of their nutrients through their diet. I add supplements to support a health or nutritional need. For example, Rodrigo gets digestive enzymes and a joint supplement because he has EPI and arthritis.

SUPPLEMENTS I ADD TO MY DOGS' DIET AND WHY

I no longer share the supplements I add to my dogs' diet because what works for my dogs may not work for your dogs.

Many people new to raw feeding think there's a list out there that tells us all of the supplements our dogs have to have. There are a lot of people who will happily sell you supplements your dog doesn't need because most people don't know any better.

If you are new to raw feeding, take some time and allow the diet to work before you start adding supplements. Or work with a meal formulator who can advise you of the appropriate supplement for your dog.

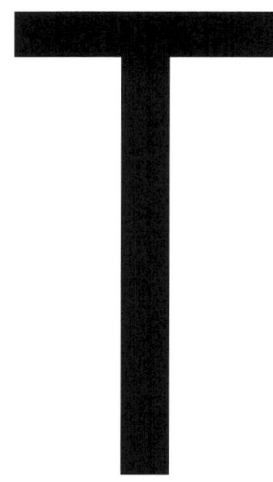

T - Transitioning Your Partner to Raw Feeding

HOW TO GET YOUR PARTNER ON BOARD WITH RAW FEEDING

My partner was hesitant about raw feeding. Today, he's 100% on board but still feels uncomfortable when I do meal prep.

I explained what I wanted to do and why and showed him what I was learning. I think he was more comfortable because we started with commercial raw. He could see the changes in Rodrigo, so when I switched to DIY, he helped me out for a few months.

Because my partner isn't comfortable with me doing meal prep in the kitchen (where the human food lives), we created space for me in the garage to do meal prep during the warmer months. During the rest of the year, I do large meal prep sessions in the dining room and smaller ones in the kitchen, and I clean every inch.

Not everyone is going to be okay with raw feeding, and it'll take some a while to get used to the idea. Be patient, but persevere.

5 THINGS NOT TO DO WHEN TRANSITIONING TO RAW

DON'T plan to feed your dog only one cut of meat. Different proteins bring different amino acid profiles and nutrients to the bowl. Shake it up.

DON'T accept raw recipes from strangers unless you are prepared to research the ingredients. Are they okay for your dog (some dogs have food sensitivities)? Can you source the ingredients, and if not, can you find acceptable substitutions? If a recipe is overly complicated, it's not a good transition recipe.

DON'T feed your dog cooked bones because they splinter and can be fatal.

DON'T allow others to scare you away from raw feeding. Whether it's veterinarians who swear raw feeding is dangerous or raw feeders who swear you're doing it wrong, don't allow others to scare you away from feeding your dog a better diet.

U - Understanding Your Dog and Raw Feeding

LET YOUR DOG BE YOUR GUIDE

My dogs will eat most everything and aren't picky. If a protein doesn't work for them, they will make it clear by stepping away after sniffing the food.

UNDERSTANDING YOUR DOG WHEN FEEDING A RAW FOOD DIET

One mistake I see many new raw feeders make is not adjusting the "rules" of raw feeding to their dogs. While it's great to learn from more experienced raw feeders, it's important to adjust some rules to meet our dogs' needs. In this post, I will share a few ways I've made the "rules" work for my dogs.

START RAW FEEDING WITH CHICKEN

The Rule: I've been told when we start feeding our dogs a raw food diet, we should start with chicken. I think this is because it's readily available, affordable, and easy for dogs to digest. I know plenty of people who feed a raw diet that is at least 50% chicken to their dogs.

My Rule: Rodrigo and Scout are allergic to chicken. Chicken promotes inflammation due to the high Omega 6 it brings to the diet. It's not the best option for dogs with food/environmental sensitivities or arthritis.

HOW MUCH I FEED OUR DOGS

The Rule: According to raw food calculators, I should feed our dogs 2.5-3% of their body weight per day; less if I want them to lose weight, more if I want them to gain weight or if they are very active.

My Rule: Rodrigo has a high metabolism, and he's an active dog; he eats almost as much food as Scout, who is ten pounds heavier

CARBS IN RAW DOG FOOD

The Rule: Some people believe we should remove all carbs from a dog's diet and disagree with adding fruits and vegetables to a dog's raw diet. Excess carbs lead to weight gain and feed cancer cells.

My Rule: While I understand the need to reduce carbs from a dog's raw diet, I don't think all carbs are bad for dogs. I avoid grains and high-starch foods in my dogs' diet.

FATS IN RAW DOG FOOD

The Rule: When I published the first version of this book, the raw feeding community was scratching their collective heads as we took in the rules about balancing fat in a dog's diet. The new information told us to match fatty acids to the right protein.

My Rule: Because I feed my dogs a variety of proteins and other foods, the fats in their diet are naturally balanced, and I don't need to take any steps in this area.

MAKE YOUR OWN RAW FEEDING RULES

I don't think we should blindly follow things we read in Facebook groups, blogs, or books. When we take the time to understand what our dogs need, we can better adapt to new information, incorporating what we're learning into our dogs' diet.

Despite how far I've come over the past nine years, I am always learning and excited when something clicks for my dogs. It can be frustrating when new information flips my diet upside down, but deep down, I know this will help me raise healthier, longer living dogs.

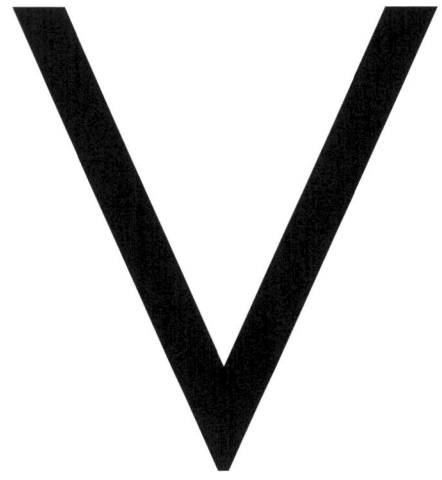

V - Vaccinations, Vegetables (and Fasting), and Raw Feeding

VACCINATIONS AND RAW FEEDING

What do vaccinations have to do with raw feeding? It was only when I started looking into feeding my dogs something different — something that would help Rodrigo's health issues — I began to learn about overvaccination and unnecessary vaccinations. These topics go hand in hand with early spay/neuter and chemical flea and tick repellents.

MY VACCINATION PROTOCOL

Because I'm not a veterinarian, I'm not going to wax philosophical about the evils of vaccinations. Instead, I'll share my thoughts on vaccinating my dogs and my protocol, which has been approved by my vet.

My dogs get their puppy vaccinations and one-year boosters. After that, my dogs are vaccinated every three or four years until they reach the age of eight. Once my dogs become seniors, they're no longer vaccinated.

I'm very conservative about vaccinations and I space out the vaccinations to decrease the chance of a negative reaction.

Titers aren't yet accepted in my state. Therefore, if I find I have to vaccinate my dogs, I will limit the vaccines to what's mandated by law, rabies. And I'll use the Leaky Gut Protocol by Adored Beast Apothecary to protect their system.

VEGETABLES AND RAW FEEDING

When I was new to raw feeding, the topic of vegetables could get you kicked out of a raw feeding group. Today, it seems to be more accepted that some of us like to feed vegetables to our dogs.

SHOULD WE FEED VEGETABLES TO DOGS?

Some people believe vegetables are just filler food and have no nutritional benefit for dogs.

Wolves shake out the stomach content of their prey, ignoring the digesting plant matter. Visit L. David Mech's site to learn more about his 40-year study of wolves in the wild: www.davemech.org/

Vegetables are difficult for dogs to digest, causing the pancreas to work too hard, leading to pancreatitis.

I disagree, sort of.

My dogs aren't wolves, and while I may take inspiration from the diet of wild dogs and wolves, this doesn't mean I won't feed vegetables. I have witnessed my dogs eating prey, and it's horrifying. They've killed their share of wild rabbits (not something I encourage), and they eat the entire rabbit. There is no shaking of the stomach contents or leaving behind the fur and skin – the entire animal goes down their gullet.

When it comes to digestion, people do have a point. Dogs don't naturally produce cellulase and can't naturally break down vegetables. However, dogs do produce amylase, which breaks down starch and carbs. The step of freezing, pureeing, or lightly cooking vegetables breaks the cellular wall allowing my dogs to better access and absorb the nutrients and fiber while removing the stress on the pancreas. I still see remnants of whole vegetables in my dogs' poop, but it doesn't all pass straight through.

WHY I FEED MY DOGS VEGETABLES

I feed my dogs vegetables because they are a great source of fiber, antioxidants, and nutrients. I feed fruit for the same reason, but I'm more conservative because of the natural sugar. Fruit is fed in the summer on high activity days when it's in season (apples, pears, blueberries, raspberries, and blackberries are favorites in our house).

I won't feed my dogs less meat when I add vegetables to the diet. Instead, I add a small amount of vegetable matter (base mix) to my meal prep, and I feed my dogs vegetables on foraging days (an idea taken from the Rotational MonoFeeding model of raw feeding).

MY DIY VEGGIE MIX

Years ago, on the advice of a holistic veterinarian, I started making a pureed veggie mix for my dogs to boost their gut health and immune system and to help one of my dogs lose weight.

My veggie mix varies based on the vegetables available at the store. I prefer low glycemic, organic vegetables and grow my own every summer. My gardens include:

- Kale
- Parsley
- Celery
- Zucchini
- Green beans
- Yellow squash
- Collard greens
- Strawberries
- Blueberries
- Apples

GENETICALLY MODIFIED VEGETABLES (GMO)

After having two cancer diagnoses, I now buy 100% organic, non-GMO vegetables and fruit when my garden is done for the year.

GARLIC FOR DOGS

Despite all the warnings, garlic is safe for many dogs to eat, and I add garlic to my dogs' diet.

- Garlic offers many benefits for dogs:
- Garlic helps to fight cancer by destroying cancer cells.

- Garlic acts as a natural detox.
- Garlic stops the formation of blood clots in the system.
- Garlic reduces cholesterol.
- Garlic is a natural antibiotic, anti-fungal, and anti-parasitic.

How much garlic is safe for dogs to consume:

- 10 to 15 pounds (4.5 to 6.8 kg) – half a clove.
- 20 to 40 pounds (9.1 to 18.1 kg) – 1 clove.
- 45 to 70 pounds (20.4 to 31.8 kg) – 2 cloves.

How to add garlic to a dog's raw diet:

- I use a supplement because it's easy.

According to Herbalist Rita Hogan in an article she wrote for Dogs Naturally Magazine, the property in garlic that provides medicinal benefits is called allicin, which degrades after a while (10-15 minutes), so it must be used immediately. Using crushed or minced garlic we find at the grocery store won't work; the medicinal benefits are no longer there. It must be fresh garlic – crush, allow to sit for 10 minutes, then mix the appropriate dosage into a dog's meal.

Although garlic is easy to grow, and I like to add it to my vegetable garden, I find it easier to add a garlic supplement to my dogs' meals to support their health and keep fleas at bay.

When we shouldn't feed garlic:

- Pregnant or lactating dogs
- Puppies (less than three months old)
- Dogs diagnosed with an anemic condition

FASTING – PLANT (VEGETABLE) DAYS

In early 2022, I was introduced to a new raw feeding model – Rotational MonoFeeding (RMF) – by Nora Lenz. This raw feeding model is discussed in more detail on my blog and earlier in this book. For this section, let's just talk about plant days.

I don't believe dogs can thrive on a plant-based diet. After a decade of learning about dogs and dog nutrition, I am well aware I don't know everything but I'm confident dogs are carnivores, not omnivores. Dogs thrive on a meat-based diet.

I also believe feeding adult dogs daily isn't good for their overall health long term. I fast my dogs at least twice a week and prefer one of those days to be a non-animal protein day. I know dogs aren't wolves and my dogs aren't wild – but I use the diet and behavior of wolves and wild dogs to inspire how I feed my dogs. And wolves and wild dogs fast, they also…

- Get a lot of daily exercise as they hunt for their prey.
- Gorge on a kill and then fast/forage for a few days.

Fasting gives the gut a break from processing the food. Because 70-80% of the gut lives in the immune system (the percentage depends on what source you're using), fasting allows the immune system to reset while the gut rests.

I feed my dogs several days a week, incorporating a full fast and a modified fast in the week.

A full fast is when my dogs don't eat anything for at least 20 hours. For example, I'll feed a heavier dinner Wednesday night, and the dogs won't eat again until the following afternoon, around 3 pm.

A modified fast is when I feed bone broth or kefir (raw goat's milk, homemade yogurt) to my dogs for the day (three meals). I began doing a modified fast to avoid hunger pukes. After learning about RMF, I sometimes feed vegetables on modified fasting days.

When it comes to fasting, you'll find many people have opinions. Some folks think it's cruel, worried we're starving our dogs – we're

not. Some people think their fasting method is the only right way –
they're wrong.

I took a lot of time testing fasting regimens with my dogs until I
settled on the above. So, please don't feel like you need to do this.

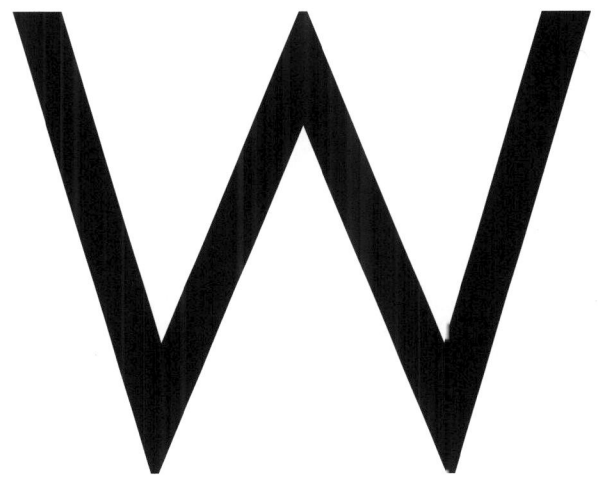

W - Warming Foods, Cooling Foods, and Raw Feeding

WARMING AND COOLING FOODS FOR DOGS

Food energetics is a practice in Traditional Chinese Medicine that states there is energy in food, and this energy affects our system in different ways.

Foods are identified as hot, warming, neutral, and cooling. This doesn't mean hot food will give you a fever or cooling food will give you chills. Instead, hot foods contribute to or exacerbate inflammation and allergies. While cooling foods reduce inflammation and calm allergies.

This is a fascinating and somewhat complicated topic. I discovered it while feeding kibble and trying to determine Rodrigo's allergies. Rodrigo is a HOT dog. Kibble is already a "hot" food because of the processing, so there was no way for me to cool it down enough to help my hot dog.

So, I switched to raw.

CHARACTERISTICS OF A HOT DOG

This is only a partial list, and not every HOT dog will exhibit all of the following characteristics. For instance, Rodrigo has a wet nose, and his paw pads are healthy.

- Lots of panting
- Sleeps next to the door and on cold tile/hardwood floors
- Active
- Drinks lots of water
- Dry nose
- Dry paw pads
- Loves the snow
- Red gums and tongue

CHARACTERISTICS OF A COLD DOG

This is only a partial list, and not every COLD dog will exhibit all of the following characteristics.

- Not a lot of panting
- Sleeps under the covers
- Sedentary
- Drinks less water
- Wet nose
- Loves the sun
- Pink gums and tongue

Because food energetics is an involved topic, I'm going to limit this section to the energy of common foods we feed to our dogs. Please remember how the animal was raised, what it was fed, and what it was exposed to can change the energy. For example, grass-fed, free-range meat will be cooler than factory-farmed meat (in tight, stressful locations, repeatedly treated with antibiotics, fed a high-grain diet).

The following labels were derived from Yin & Yang Nutrition for Dogs by Dr. Judy Morgan. I also refer to the charts published by Herbsmith LLC, a supplement company, and Dr. Doug Knueven.

PROTEINS

- Alligator – cooling
- Beef – neutral
- Beef liver – neutral
- Bison – neutral
- Carp – neutral
- Cheese – neutral
- Chicken – warming
- Chicken eggs (pasture-raised) – neutral
- Duck – cooling
- Duck eggs – cooling
- Emu – hot

- Goat's milk – warming
- Goose (wild) – cooling
- Herring – cooling
- Lamb – hot
- Mackerel – neutral
- Mussels – cooling
- Oysters – cooling
- Pheasant – warming
- Pork – cooling/neutral
- Quail – neutral
- Rabbit – cooling
- Wild salmon – neutral
- Sardines – neutral
- Shrimp – hot
- Tripe (beef) – neutral
- Trout* – neutral/hot
- Turkey (wild) – cooling/neutral
- Turkey (farmed) – warming
- Venison – hot
- Whitefish – cooling

VEGETABLES

- Alfalfa – cooling
- Asparagus – cooling
- Broccoli – cooling
- Cabbage – neutral
- Carrots – neutral
- Cauliflower – neutral
- Celery – cooling
- Cucumber – cooling
- Garlic – warming
- Green beans – neutral
- Mushrooms* – cooling (Shiitake mushrooms are neutral)
- Pumpkin – warming
- Spinach* – cooling
- Squash – warming

- Sweet Potatoes – neutral/warming
- Yams – neutral

* I feed store bought mushrooms to my dogs (brown, Portobello, Reiki, Shiitake); not mushrooms picked in our yard. If a dog is prone to stones, high oxalate foods, like spinach, should be limited (or removed) from the diet. And, some of the foods are labeled with two energies; I noted them both.

FRUIT

- Apple – cooling
- Banana – cooling
- Blueberries – cooling
- Honey – cooling
- Pear – cooling
- Persimmons – cooling
- Raspberry – warming
- Strawberry – cooling
- Watermelon – cooling

HOW I USE FOOD ENERGETICS

I turn to food energetics to treat health issues. Rodrigo has environmental allergies, so I cool down the "hot" proteins with "cooling" foods. And I don't feed "hot" proteins in the summer – he's already hot enough.

I didn't even scratch the surface here, and I'm still learning. Dr. Judy Morgan is brilliant on this subject.

X - Examining Dog Poop and Raw Feeding

RAW FEEDERS ARE OBSESSED WITH DOG POOP

A daily chore at my house is cleaning up the dog yard, which is also a great opportunity to see how the dogs are doing. It started with Rodrigo because he's had gut issues from the beginning.

Monitoring their stool has taught me…

- How my dog poops (pile or trail).
- How often my dog poops.
- If I need to add more bone to the diet.
- If I need to add less organ meat to the diet.
- How quickly my dogs digest proteins.
- How quickly my dogs digest vegetables.
- If a protein or herb is a bad fit.
- If my dog has any reactions to medicines.

If one of my dogs has diarrhea that doesn't clear up in a couple of days, I call the veterinarian. If there's a lot of mucus on the stool, I'll start examining their diet for what could be irritating their gut.

These aren't the only solutions, just a start.

HOME REMEDIES FOR DIARRHEA

My dogs rarely get diarrhea, and when it does happen, it usually clears up in a day. I keep several natural options on hand as home remedies:

- **organic canned pumpkin**
- **organic canned sweet potato**
- **slippery elm**
- **Olewo Carrots**
- **Organic fiber**
- **Treats with fur** (cow ears, rabbit feet, rabbit ears)*

*I only feed fur as an occasional treat because I question the nutritional benefits and I'm concerned about the risk of a blockage because too much fur may be difficult for my dogs to digest.

111

Disclaimer: I am not a veterinarian or a nutritionist.

When it comes to diarrhea, please keep your veterinarian in the loop. If you don't see improvement within 24 hours of using a home remedy, it's time to call the vet.

Y - YouTube Channels for Raw Feeders

YOUTUBE IS AN EXCELLENT RESOURCE FOR RAW FEEDERS

If you're a person who learns through observation, YouTube is an excellent resource. Many raw feeders are sharing what they feed their dogs and any health issues that are cured or crop up. Some raw feeders go further by demonstrating meal prep, shopping trips, and more in their videos.

I don't count on these videos to provide nutritionally complete meals; instead, I look to these videos for information on raw feeding, meal prep tips, and ideas on different foods I can add to my dogs' diet.

I think it's important to follow various raw feeding channels (or channels that discuss raw feeding) to gain a variety of methods.

One channel that consistently puts out quality information about raw feeding is **Paws of Prey**. But if you search "**raw food dog**," you'll find a lot of interesting videos.

And, you can find me on YouTube by searching "**Kimberly Gauthier**," or "**Keep the Tail Wagging**."

Z - The Zen of a Full Freezer, Buying a Freezer, and Forgetting to Thaw Raw Dog Food

I LOVE AN ORGANIZED FREEZER

There's nothing like having a full freezer, especially when most of my meal prep is complete. We have two dedicated freezers and a fridge for our dogs (in the garage) because I order in bulk and need the extra space.

Ordering through a local raw food co-op allows me to order what I need by the case, and the additional freezers are home to cases of duck, pork heart, bison and lamb bones, whole quail, and more. Having dedicated freezers allows me to take advantage of specials, and stock up on products that are set to change, be discontinued, or go up in price.

BUYING ADDITIONAL FREEZERS

When I was first in the market for a new freezer, I stopped by a few stores to see how much they cost and was stunned by the prices. Thankfully, here in Western Washington, you can find great deals on refurbished appliances at the Appliance Recycling Outlet in Snohomish, Washington.

I prefer to buy refurbished instead of used because a refurbished freezer has been serviced, may come with a warranty, and I'm confident it works without increasing our electricity bill.

I look for freezers with adjustable shelves, space in the door, and drawers at the bottom. I want a freezer with plenty of space for hundreds of pounds of raw dog food.

STAND-UP VS. CHEST FREEZERS

I prefer stand-up freezers because they are easier to organize. However, a friend recently gave me a tip for organizing a chest freezer. She uses milk crates to keep them organized – one crate for bones, one crate for green tripe, etc.

Dedicated freezers aren't a requirement for raw feeding, so if you don't have the space for one, don't worry about it.

I FORGOT TO THAW RAW MEALS FOR MY DOGS!!!

It happens all the time. I bolt awake at 4 am and realize I forgot to thaw meals for my dogs. This would send me into a panic years ago, but today, it's no big deal. We have options.

When I forget to thaw food for my dogs, I do one of the following:

1 – I HAVE AN IMPROMPTU FASTING DAY.

I'll take some food out of the freezer, something quick and easy, along with a regular DIY meal, and start thawing. For my dogs, green tripe is quick and easy to thaw, so they'll have green tripe later that day (or the next day).

I make of point of always keeping raw goat's milk, kefir, or bone broth thaws in the freezer and can add those to the bowl if I don't want to do a full fast.

2 – PUZZLE TOGETHER A MEAL.

I keep lean, grass-fed ground beef on hand as a backup and I add the following:

- a base mix
- scrambled or poached eggs
- canned sardines and oysters
- bone broth

I also keep at least ten pounds of **Darwin's Pet** food on hand. It thaws quickly in a sink of warm water.

3 – HEAD TO THE GROCERY STORE.

My local grocery store has a section of discounted, soon-to-expire meat. I buy the leanest cuts of meat and make dehydrated dog treats or add them to meals as a "side dish."

I add the ingredients listed above, and I have a solid meal without breaking the bank. These meals aren't "balanced," but they're healthy and fine to feed in a pinch. And, since I balance my adult dogs' diets over time, I'm confident I'm meeting their nutritional needs.

What if My Dog Won't Eat Raw?

IF A DOG WON'T EAT RAW

When I was new to raw, I was like a Born Again Christian and proselytized to anyone and everyone with a dog because I was convinced raw feeding was the answer to everything.

Over the years, I've learned raw feeding isn't for everyone or every dog, and that's okay.

If your dog isn't down with raw feeding, there are many ways to improve your dog's diet. And I have first-hand experience with a dog that won't eat raw.

In late 2021, Rodrigo began shying away from raw meals, and I later learned this is common with senior dogs. I made the following changes:

- I began warming up his food. This intensifies the yummy smells and makes the food easier to digest because his system doesn't have to work to bring the food to room temperature.
- I started feeding cooked dog food. Sometimes his reluctance was the temperature; other times, it was the texture. Cooked food has a texture he likes.
- I ordered commercial raw and cooked food for him. There are a couple of brands (one raw, one gently cooked) Rodrigo enjoys, and I began ordering small amounts and adding them to the rotation.
- I feed freeze-dried dog food to him on occasion. There are several brands available with a variety of proteins.

Rodrigo returned to eating raw in late 2022.

Easy
Supplemental
Recipes
for Dogs

DIY BONE BROTH

Bone broth is fantastic for the immune system, digestive system, and joints. I make a batch at least once a month to add to my dogs' food or feed as a frozen treat in the summer.

BENEFITS OF BONE BROTH FOR DOGS:

- Supports gut health; promotes a healthy digestive system
- Supports joint health
- Promotes the body's natural detox (great for liver and kidneys)
- Excellent for sick dogs (easy on the tummy)
- Excellent for picky dogs (makes meals smell yummy)

The following recipe is made in an 8-quart pressure cooker and can be adjusted based on your equipment.

INGREDIENTS (these vary based on what's available):

- Bones (turkey legs, chicken legs, pork ribs, lamb necks, beef or bison stock bones, or sardines/fish heads)
- Apple cider vinegar
- 5-8 cloves (not bulbs) of fresh garlic (optional)
- Kale, dandelion greens, or turmeric (optional)

EQUIPMENT:

- Slow cooker (takes 24 hours) or pressure cooker (takes 4-5 hours)
- Spoon with a ladle or mesh colander (to strain out bones)
- Glass jars

DIRECTIONS:

I fill my pressure cooker (or slow cooker) with bones and add enough water to cover the bones. I add 1/4 cup of apple cider vinegar and the garlic cloves. Cook until finished (slow cooker takes 24 hours; my pressure cooker takes 3-4 hours).

I allow the bone broth to cool for two hours or overnight.

I strain the bones (keep the meat in broth) from the broth and transfer the broth into glass jars to store in the freezer for later use.

I do not buy broth from the grocery store because I don't know what bones were used, the sodium levels seem too high, and many brands add onions, which aren't healthy for dogs.

GARLIC:

I do add garlic to my dogs' diet. I prefer using Bug Off granules by Springtime Supplements. Garlic has many health benefits and the amount I add to my bone broth isn't close to the toxic levels we were warned about.

I do not feed garlic (or add it to my bone broth) when we have a puppy in the crew. I would also skip this ingredient any of my dogs were living with an anemic condition.

SARDINE BONE BROTH:

I make sardine bone broth in a slow cooker because I don't want my pressure cooker to smell like fish. It only takes a few hours, and I cook it outside.

After two or three hours of cooking in a slow cooker, I strain the fish and bones, allow the broth to cool, then transfer the broth to wide-mouth jars. I freeze the broth until I need it.

I puree the fish and bones into a mush and transfer it to smaller jars and freeze it for later use.

TURMERIC PASTE AKA GOLDEN PASTE

I began making golden paste for my dogs to ease joint pain. Today, I add to all of their meals because it has so many more benefits.

BENEFITS OF GOLDEN PASTE FOR DOGS:

This is a short list of the benefits of golden paste for dogs:

- Natural detox
- Anti-inflammatory
- Natural antibacterial
- Promotes heart and liver health
- Reduces blood clots that can lead to strokes and heart attacks by thinning the blood
- Promotes digestive health
- Acts as an antioxidant AND it's believed to be able to prevent cancer
- Offers allergy relief
- Helps to prevent cataracts
- Has been used in the treatment of epilepsy
- Natural pain relief
- Natural treatment for diarrhea

INGREDIENTS:

- 3 cups of turmeric powder (I order through our co-op)
- 6 cups of water
- 2 cups of organic coconut oil (or 1 cup of coconut oil and 1 cup of bone broth)
- 3 tablespoons of freshly ground pepper (from a pepper mill)
- 2 tablespoons of Ceylon cinnamon

EQUIPMENT:

- Saucepan
- Stove
- Spoon
- Whisk

124

-   Glass jars

DIRECTIONS:

Step 1: I slowly warm the water on the lowest heat while I ground the pepper I need.

Step 2: I mix the turmeric powder in with the water and stir until it begins to get thick.

Step 3: I mix in the coconut oil and bone broth, and, finally, the pepper. I turn off the heat and continue to stir.

Step 4: I allow the turmeric paste to cool and transfer it into Rubbermaid containers to freeze.

I make my golden paste in large batches, storing the excess in the freezer. It is good in the fridge for two weeks.

TURMERIC PASTE DOSAGE FOR DOGS

I've read different dosages on several sites. Many people advise starting with small amounts and building up because it can cause loose stool if you feed too much to your dog. Turmeric paste leaves a dog's system quickly, so it should be fed with each meal.

I started my dogs off with 1/4 teaspoon in each meal and worked up to gauge their tolerance. Ultimately, you want to do 1/4 teaspoon for every 10 pounds of body weight.

-   Start by adding 1/4 – 1/2 teaspoon of golden paste to each meal
-   Every 5-7 days, increase the dosage a small amount

Once you notice pain relief, increased mobility, or a decrease in tumor size (yeah, I read this could happen, and I'm blown away) — you've found your maintenance dosage.

For dogs that don't have any pre-existing health issues (joints and digestive), I stick with the lower dosage of 1/4 – 1/2 teaspoon per meal because more gives them diarrhea.

VEGGIE MIX

Years ago, my veterinarian recommended adding more vegetables to my dogs' diet when I was helping Sydney lose weight. He gave me a list of vegetables and fruit that were a good fit for my dogs, and I created a vegetable puree.

BENEFITS OF VEGETABLES FOR DOGS:

While some raw feeders don't believe vegetables are a natural part of a dog's diet, I disagree. There is evidence wolves do eat plant material - when foraging and to correct their microbiome.

- Vegetables provide antioxidants that are known to fight off cancer.
- Vegetables help balance a dog's system, keeping it from being too acidic or too alkaline.
- Vegetables provide additional nutrients when fed pureed or fermented.
- Fermented vegetables offer a natural source of probiotics; Note: the below recipe isn't for fermented vegetables.
- Vegetables provide fiber to help with digestion.
- Vegetables can help an overweight dog feel full when on a diet.

INGREDIENTS (these vary based on what's available):

I source most of my organic vegetables and fruits from the grocery store. I alternate the vegetables I add, only using two greens. I only add spinach if I grow it myself or get it from a friend's garden. Commercial spinach is treated with potent pesticides.

- 2 bundles of kale

- 2 bundles of collard greens
- 2 bundles of parsley
- 4 zucchinis (6 if they're small)
- 1 or 2 celery leaf stalks (not the individual celery) • 2 or 3 apples
- 1 package of blueberries
- 5 cloves of fresh garlic (see Letter V to learn more)
- 1 or 2 packages of freeze-dried mushrooms — shiitake, cremini, portobello (optional)
- 1 inch of ginger (optional)
- Apple cider vinegar (optional)
- Bone broth (optional)
- Turmeric paste (optional)

EQUIPMENT:

- Blender or food processor
- Knife
- Cutting board
- Large stainless-steel bowls
- Large spoon or ladle for mixing
- Glass jars or ice cube trays

DIRECTIONS:

I chop up the vegetables and fruit to make it easier to puree in the blender. Buying organic greens (kale, spinach, etc.) from Costco can save you time during this step.

I fill each large bowl with the blended vegetables and fruit, leaving room to add bone broth and turmeric paste.

I pour the mixture into glass jars or ice cube trays to freeze.

If you don't have time to make bone broth, there is premade bone broth available at some local pet stores. I do not buy broth from the grocery store because many brands add onions and the sodium level is too high for my dogs (personal opinion).

FERMENTED VEGETABLES

A few years after I began making my veggie mix, I began to wonder if it would be better to ferment vegetables. It's an easy process, and I fermented vegetables for a few years.

BENEFITS OF FERMENTED FOOD FOR DOGS:

Easy to Digest: Fermented foods are easier to digest and don't make the gut work hard to break down and absorb the nutrients in the food.

Probiotics: Fermented foods provide healthy, natural probiotics for gut health. And because this is a natural source of probiotics, it may replace commercial supplements for many dogs, saving us money. Not only are fermented vegetables a source of probiotics, but the vegetables also act as food for the gut's bacteria population.

Improved Immune System: Fermented foods help improve gut health, which frees up the immune system to do its job, helping to decrease allergies and inflammation. Healthy gut, healthy dog!

Antioxidants Fight Cancer: Fermented vegetables are an excellent source of fiber, antioxidants, and phytonutrients (a substance found in many plants that supports good health and prevents disease).

I follow a recipe from the Canine Ascension Facebook page. The first time, I only used one green cabbage, one red cabbage, and one carrot. The second time, I got a little more creative.

This recipe produced eight jars of fermented vegetables. I have four dogs, and we'll go through these vegetables quickly (plus, I eat them too).

INGREDIENTS (these vary based on what's available):

- 2 bundles of kale or collard greens (I prefer collard greens)
- 1 green cabbage
- 1 red cabbage

- 5 small zucchinis
- 1 bundle of asparagus
- 2-1/2 tbsp of sea salt (don't use table salt)
- water (as needed)

Remember you can make fermented vegetables using two heads of cabbage and 1 tbsp of sea salt. If this is your first time, I recommend starting small and building up. For me, this created three jars of fermented vegetables.

EQUIPMENT:

- **Easy Fermenter Set (Lids and Pump)**
- **Easy Fermenter Weights**
- **Packer (optional)**
- **Ball Wide Mouth Mason Jars**
- **Stainless Steel Bowls**

DIRECTIONS:

Peel the top layer of leaves from the cabbages and set them aside for use later.

Chop up all the vegetables as finely as possible; the list of vegetables above will fill two 8-quart stainless steel bowls. If you only use two heads of cabbage, you'll fill one 8-quart stainless steel bowl.

Add 1-1/4 tbsp of freshly ground sea salt to each bowl and massage the vegetables until they become wet (add 1 tbsp if only two heads of cabbage). The salt helps to bring the water out of the vegetables, which will be the brine to help ferment. The salt also serves as food for the bacteria (very little salt remains when the fermentation is complete).

Allow the bowls to sit for 20 minutes, then massage the vegetables again. You'll notice the vegetables seem to be shrinking and liquid (this is your brine) begins to collect at the bottom of the bowl. I started with a bowl overflowing with vegetables, and after massaging twice, there were 3 inches of room at the top of each bowl.

Repeat the message/sit for one or two more times; if there isn't a good amount of liquid (the brine) in the bottom of the bowl (see video below), then add a small amount of water.

Spoon the vegetables into each jar, using a large, flexible spoon to press the vegetables down. This removes any air pockets and makes room for more vegetables. You can also purchase a packer (see list above) to help with this step.

When the vegetables are evenly distributed and packed down tight, add the cabbage leaves (pack down again) and add one weight per jar. Seal each jar with the Easy Fermenter lids (see list above).

Ferment vegetables for 20 days (10 days in the summer); the Easy Fermenter lids allow you to set the date when the fermentation is complete. I use the pump in the kit to remove any excess air each week until the vegetables are ready; this is optional.

ISN'T SALT BAD FOR DOGS?

The salt used to ferment vegetables helps to bring the liquid out of the vegetables and serves as food for the growing bacteria that ferments the vegetables. When the vegetables are ready, they taste amazing - you won't be able to taste the salt. This small amount of salt isn't bad for dogs or humans; excess salt is something we want to avoid.

HOW DO I KNOW WHEN THE FERMENTATION IS DONE?

The beauty of the Easy Fermenter system is it's super easy. Dialing to the date the ferment is done is when the ferment is done.

- 20 days during cooler months
- 10 days during hotter months

When determining if your ferment is done, look for activity (bubbles). If there are bubbles in an airtight container after the time period listed above, allow to sit for a few more days. If there are no bubbles, your ferment is done.

WILL MY DOGS EAT FERMENTED VEGETABLES?

I can't promise your dogs will eat fermented vegetables. Hence, if you'd like to try it out, I recommend buying them in the refrigerated section of a local natural grocery store. I tried Bubbies and Firefly Kitchens with my dogs. Avoid fermented vegetables with onions.

Or you can make a test batch and see how they like them.

FEEDING GUIDELINES FOR FERMENTED VEGETABLES

Some people believe 20% or more of a dog's diet should be vegetation. I think this is too much (personal opinion) and feed between 5-10% to my dogs.

I feed my dogs one tablespoon (usually a heaping spoonful) of fermented vegetables per meal.

If your dog is new to eating fermented vegetables, start small and work your way up to allow their gut to get used to this new treat. And if your dog will not eat the fermented vegetables, no worries, there are other options: raw goat's milk, kefir, and fermented fish bone broth/stock.

FREEZING FERMENTED VEGETABLES

Once the ferment is complete, I move a couple of jars to the fridge and the rest to a cold area (garage or cellar). The cold temperatures slow the fermentation. I've read fermented vegetables can be stored for up to a year; however, my concern is that the probiotics won't remain viable for twelve months, so I only freeze them for a month. Once opened, I keep them in the fridge for up to two weeks.

You can freeze fermented vegetables; simply transfer the contents of the jar to a freezer-safe container for freezing. While the fridge or cold storage slows the fermentation, freezing stops it.

Read: Fermenting Veggies FAQs by FermentedFoodLab.com for answers to more questions.

131

If you're interested in fermenting seeds, read Canine Ascension's post.

Read: Recipe for Fermenting Seeds for Dogs.

HISTAMINES IN FERMENTED FOODS

I've read fermented foods are high in histamines and shouldn't be fed to dogs prone to allergies or yeast issues. I think every pet parent should do what's right for their dog. However, I've been told by an expert in fermentation that the amount of histamines in fermented foods is negligible and won't cause an issue.

WHY I NO LONGER FERMENT VEGETABLES

I no longer ferment vegetables because it takes a lot of time, and my dogs get plenty of fermented foods – raw goat's milk, kefir, yogurt, and fermented fish stock/broth.

DIY YOGURT

ARE DOGS LACTOSE INTOLERANT?

Yes, dogs can eat yogurt. In my reading, I learned to go slowly when adding yogurt to the diet to see how the dog responds. Dogs that are lactose intolerant may be able to consume cheese and yogurt without issue. Pasteurized milk and possibly raw cow's milk (because it contains more lactose than raw goat's milk) are the issues.

You can tell if your dog is lactose intolerant because after consuming dairy, your dog may experience bloating, gas, loose stool, diarrhea, and a sensitive (uncomfortable) tummy.

My dogs do great on cow or goat kefir and raw goat's milk because both are unprocessed and low in lactose, making them easier to digest. I feed my dogs a meal of raw goat's milk and/or kefir (sometimes I mix the two - to make the milk creamier).

BENEFITS OF YOGURT FOR DOGS

Yogurt offers the same benefits as raw goat's milk and kefir for dogs. It supports digestive health by adding beneficial bacteria to the gut while also supporting the immune system. So, if we can give these benefits to our dogs through raw goat's milk and kefir, then why add yogurt?

- yogurt is rich in probiotics, supporting gut health and the immune system
- yogurt is a great protein source
- yogurt is rich in vitamin B
- yogurt adds a little bit of calcium to the diet
- adds variety to the diet
- yogurt is a substitute if a dog can't have raw goat's milk or kefir
- if you don't have a source for raw goat's milk or kefir, try or make yogurt (recipes below)

With the supply chain slowdown, I've lost easy access to raw goat's milk. I had one source locally with fewer goats. And my second source, a commercial raw brand I ordered by the case, changed their sourcing, changing the quality of their products. Thankfully, I stocked up on raw goat's milk and kefir and now have a freezer full.

But what happens when my stock dwindles and I haven't found a source that is good enough? Maybe yogurt is the answer.

IS YOGURT A GOOD SOURCE OF CALCIUM FOR DOGS?

No. I don't believe we can feed enough yogurt for it to cover a dog's daily requirement for calcium. Other bone substitutes include eggshells, seaweed calcium, or a quality supplement. Speak with an animal nutritionist for amounts.

IS YOGURT A GOOD SOURCE OF PROBIOTICS FOR DOGS?

Maybe. If I couldn't feed my dogs raw goat's milk or kefir, I would add another fermented food or an organic fiber supplement to their diet. I believe yogurt can provide more strains of probiotics than many probiotic supplements for dogs. Plus, I can vary the strains with each batch.

Conversely, yogurt doesn't contain the prebiotics and digestive enzymes that are also present in the supplements offered by Adored Beast Apothecary. But those things can be provided by other foods:

- Whole food sources of prebiotics: flaxseed, dandelion greens, and seaweed
- Whole food sources of probiotics: raw goat's milk, kefir, yogurt, fermented foods (vegetables, fish broth)

WHICH TYPE OF YOGURT IS BEST FOR DOGS?

I also learned three yogurts are recommended for dogs:

- Plain yogurt, with no fruit or artificial sweeteners, is recommended because it contains more probiotics that are healthy for dogs.
- Greek yogurt, with no fruit or artificial sweeteners, is recommended because it contains more probiotics that are healthy for dogs.
- Homemade yogurt is recommended because we can control the ingredients and processing.

If given the choice to buy yogurt or make the yogurt in my pressure cooker, I'd prefer DIY. It's less expensive, and I don't always know which brand is the best. If you plan to buy yogurt, ensure it contains live cultures and little sugar.

DIY YOGURT FOR DOGS [INSTANT POT RECIPE]

Three things I learned when reading about how to make yogurt were:

- it's very easy to make and hard to mess up
- the bacteria in the raw milk might compete with the bacteria in the starter
- it's okay to use raw goat's milk

INGREDIENTS:
134

- a yogurt starter (living bacteria that turns milk into yogurt)
- raw goat's milk

EQUIPMENT:

- Instant Pot
- Wide-Mouth Jars

DIRECTIONS:

PART ONE

- Clean your Instant Pot thoroughly so the yogurt doesn't take on the taste of the last thing you cooked (i.e., bone broth).
- Pour about 1/2 gallon of organic whole milk into the Instant Pot.
- Add 1/2 cup of plain organic milk.
- Mix thoroughly with a wire whisk.
- Add lid and seal; set Instant Pot to Yogurt for six hours.

PART TWO

- Open the lid and happily look at your creamy creation.
- Transfer to two wide-mouth glass jars and refrigerate.
- Yogurt can be stored in the fridge for one to two weeks.
- Fresh yogurt does freeze well.

MY Final Thoughts on RAW FEEDING

MY FINAL THOUGHTS ON RAW FEEDING

OVERCOMPLICATING RAW FEEDING

When I was new to raw feeding, I quickly became overwhelmed. So many people told me raw feeding is easy and fun, but without the support of the veterinarian community, I didn't believe them. This drove me to cover all my bases to prove to veterinarians I was doing it right.

This was stressful and expensive. I was tempted to return to feeding kibble many times. Thankfully, I pushed through because I believe raw feeding is what gave me a great final summer with Sydney and more than 520 days with Scout after he was diagnosed with cancer. And I know raw feeding is why Rodrigo is still with us despite the prognosis that we'd lose him shortly after his third birthday.

THE MONETIZATION OF RAW FEEDING

In 2018, I noticed a shift in the raw feeding community. While the passion and 'my way or the highway' mindsets have always been a part of our community, things were changing. People were monetizing raw feeding.

Today, people earn money through meal formulation and coaching services, allowing pet parents to feed nutritionally complete meals and get veterinarians on the side of raw feeding.

With these services, we're seeing a rise in competition and the growing belief DIY raw feeding cannot meet a dog's nutritional needs. I disagree.

RAW FEEDING CAN BE EASY (AND FUN)

As a pet parent raising multiple dogs, working a full-time job, and building a side gig - I don't have time for complicated. This book shares the path I've walked that has led me to an easy meal prep routine and taught me how to better understand canine nutrition and health.

If you want to count calories, balance to NRC, or work with a meal formulator - then this is exactly what you should do. But this isn't a "rule." As you walk your path, you'll discover that what works for others may not work for your dog (and vice versa). So give yourself some grace and enjoy this time learning more about your dog.

When I said "goodbye" to Sydney and Scout, I didn't have any doubts I had given them the best life, which includes their diet. I knew I did all I could for them, and we saw the benefits every day of their lives.

KIBBLE COMPANIES WILL START MAKING RAW

This may sound like a conspiracy theory, but I think I'm on to something. We will soon see a day when one of the big kibble companies will either buy a raw food brand or come out with some kind of fresh food product to take advantage of the rising demand.

This demand has been growing for some time and the normalization of social media has allowed the benefits of raw feeding to reach more dog owners.

I believe these large companies will create a "safe" raw food or fresh food product and transition their current customers.

The food will have questionable sourcing and will be full of synthetic ingredients, and it'll be their version of "raw."

Thanks for reading.

And, thanks for your help, Kara.

Made in United States
Troutdale, OR
08/15/2023

12091773R00082